How to be Debt Free

A Proven Strategy to Take Control of Your Financial Freedom by Getting Rid of Debt, Loans, Student Loans Repayment, Credit Card Debt, Mortgages and More

Complete Volume

By

Income Mastery

How to be Debt Free

*A Proven Strategy to Take Control of Your Financial Freedom
by Getting Rid of Debt, Loans, Student Loans Repayment,
Credit Card Debt, Mortgages and More*

Volume 1

How to be Debt Free

*A Proven Strategy to Take Control of Your Financial Freedom
by Getting Rid of Debt, Loans, Student Loans Repayment,
Credit Card Debt, Mortgages and More*

Volume 2

How to be Debt Free

*A Proven Strategy to Take Control of Your Financial Freedom
by Getting Rid of Debt, Loans, Student Loans Repayment,
Credit Card Debt, Mortgages and More*

Volume 3

competence. There are no scenarios in which the publisher or author of this book can be held responsible for any difficulties or damages that may occur to them after making the information presented here.

In addition, the information on the following pages is intended for informational purposes only and should therefore be regarded as universal. As befits its nature, it is presented without warranty with respect to its prolonged validity or provisional quality. The trademarks mentioned are made without written consent and can in no way be considered as sponsorship of the same.

TABLE OF CONTENTS

How to be Debt Free: Volume 1

A Proven Strategy to Take Control of Your Financial Freedom by Getting Rid of Debt, Loans, Student Loans Repayment, Credit Card Debt, Mortgages and More

By

Income Mastery

INTRODUCTION

**"It's impossible to grow and prosper without
making more investment."**

MBA Managerial Encyclopedia

Have you ever wondered what the real concept of debt is?

Today, many people live in what is known as "the uncertainty of money"; the poor and middle class lived under certain rules of money and, although it is regrettable to say so, currently it is like that. After the uncertainty of what may happen, people are acting and living financially according to the old rule of "study an important career, work hard to earn a good salary, save money and spend it". Apart from the fact that this system does not currently work, the calmness behind the lack of progress has led new generations to save incompetently, people are sitting on a sack of money while they think they are saving it for their benefit or waiting for the situation they are living in now to stabilize, and on the other hand there are those who are "saving to spend later" without understanding that savings lose value, especially when inflation comes and grows faster than interest paid on savings accounts.

If we analyze this last point with a little discretion and attention, we might ask ourselves: So, is there some benefit in credit cards, bank credits and many other loans? The answer is yes, but only if you handle money with financial intelligence.

All this time we have been led to believe that this is the right way to do things, get a good job, be promoted, obtain a credit for a house and a car, buy "toys and whims" in installments or by bank financing, pay the minimum of credit cards to make you pay more money of the month or simply not get into debt with anything, because money is not good and "rich people do not have debts", but in reality it is not like that.

The way we invest and spend our money has a lot to do with the way we live and see the world, it even has to do with the way we perceive and project ourselves into the future. It is important to emphasize that although the technique of "working for something I want until I get it" does work, the results are short term and many times the cons are much more than we think; like how not to be comfortable with your work, not get the full money, to have a bad work experience or simply, notice that the satisfaction for had obtained what you wanted did not last as long as you expected and, among so many other things we will be thinking and acting like poor people, even though our house is full of those small "sacrifices turned into successes".

For many years we have been taught that the right way to have money is not having debts or that rich people are rich because they do not have debt, but what would happen if you figured out that all this is a myth, that money and some credits are not bad and that there are good debts and bad debts. Would you begin to invest intelligently and acquire some debts with an investor's conscience and eyesight? If your answer is yes, the information found in this book will help you to clarify any doubts you may have about money, initiate a strategy that will bring you closer every day to your financial freedom and overcome bad debts and not to be afraid of the good ones, because a rich person never loses the opportunity to take calculated risks.

Before beginning this financial journey where you will eliminate myths, taboos and certain outdated concepts regarding money, debts and their variants, it is important that you know the meaning of some key terms that will facilitate you the reading and understanding of this book.

Money: A mean of exchange, usually in the form of banknotes and coins, which is accepted by a company as payment of goods, services and all kinds of obligations. Its etymological origin leads us to the Latin word *denarius*, which was the name of the currency used by the Romans. *-Definition (website)*

Passive Income: Income generated without having to work for them, for example, income generated by real estate for rent, for businesses where we do not have to be present, or for paper assets such as stocks or bonds.
-Robert Kiyosaki

Earned Income: Income generated when we work for them, for example, by having a job, or a business that depends on our physical presence.
-Robert Kiyosaki

Assets: Anything that generates passive income for us, that is, anything that generates a cash flow for us, for example, a property in rent, a business where we don't have to be present, or a portfolio of shares.
-Robert Kiyosaki

Passive: Everything that generates expenses or makes us lose money.
Robert Kiyosaki

Cash flow quadrant: A quadrant that shows four different types of people according to the income they earn; they can be: employee (E), self-employed (A), business owner or entrepreneur (D), and investor (I).
Robert Kiyosaki

Leverage: That which allows us to make money significantly; there can be asset leverage, labor leverage, and financial leverage.
Robert Kiyosaki

Money Speed: The speed at which money invested in one asset is recouped and then invested in another.
Robert Kiyosaki

Loan: At the financial level, it is money that is requested or requested in a bank or similar entity. When you buy it, you have to repay it with interest.
Definition (website)

Bad Debt: Debt that we pay.
Robert Kiyosaki

Good Debt: Debt that someone else pays for us, for example, for a rental property, the bank gives us the loan, but our tenant pays for it.
Robert Kiyosaki

Credit Bureau: is a private, non-governmental company that receives information from banks and financial institutions that grant loans to a natural or legal person. This information is stored in a credit history under the name of the person who requested it and in this way information is collected on each credit you acquire, its payments and debts.
-Iofacturo.mx (website)

Financial intelligence: That part of our intelligence we use to solve money problems is simply to have more options.
-Robert Kiyosaki

Financial freedom: A financial concept defined as the ability to stop working and continue generating income without the person's physical presence, and to obtain freedom of time, freedom of movement, and freedom of decision, basically achieved when your passive income (income that does not depend on your job) is greater than your expenses.

Robert Kiyosaki and Camilo Cruz

"Financial education nurtures financial intelligence that leads to financial freedom."

Book Rich Father Poor Father, Robert Kiyosaki

MONEY CALLS MONEY

There are multiple beliefs about money, some managed by poor minds (intelligent, studied people who sell their time in exchange for money to acquire liabilities that look like assets) and others by wealthy minds (people who are financially educated, are not afraid to take risks, see opportunities in debt and are always looking for ways to invest in assets). It remains for us to know which to follow, the point now is to know how to differentiate which is a limiting belief in front of money and abundance and which is not.

T. Harv Eker says that we have a relationship with money that is formed many times from 0 to 7 years at an early age or later when we have a very specific situation in our money-related lives.

To determine the status of our relationship to money, it is best to carefully evaluate our thoughts and how we manage our income and expenses. This exercise will allow us to know our thought patterns, so that once we become aware of them, we can work on them.

This means that our relationship with money is influenced by everything we saw, heard and felt that it had a strong emotional charge in our life, so if you want to improve your relationship with money and make it flow abundantly in your life you must pay attention and work on a new schedule. To do this, the first thing we must do is to identify our limiting beliefs and then devote ourselves to finding examples of people who have money and who are extraordinary.

Some of the limiting beliefs we've grown up with can be:

1. If I have money, I'm gonna change and my family's gonna walk away.
2. If I have money, people don't really love me.
3. If I have money, I'm less spiritual.
4. Money connects with unhappiness and loneliness.
5. Money doesn't buy happiness.
6. The rich were born rich or they're lucky and I'm not.
7. It is better to work for something safe and a good salary than to take risks in the unknown.
8. Having a lot of material things makes me more important, no matter how I acquired them.
9. It is better never to get into debt before falling into a credit bureau.
10. "I prefer to be poor but honest," which in my opinion is the worst of all the previous ones, it's as if that means that having money can't be synonymous with honest and honest with the way we earn

money, and basically translates into "I don't deserve it".

Definitely, our relationship with money and the way it flows and influences our lives and our pockets has a lot to do with reflecting what we think, feel and say about it. Believing firmly in a universe of abundance and that we are the reflection of our thoughts and feelings, being then creators of our realities, is one of the first steps to attract money in a positive way in our lives and lead us towards the path of financial freedom.

Congruent with the steps to follow, once we recognize our limiting beliefs, organize and visualize our income and expenditures, and are willing to attract money, we begin with the part of following the people who are in the place where I want to go, from level one "I am able to get out of my debts and transform" to the maximum level "No matter if I work or not, money works for me constantly".

Tatiana Arias, one of the personalities who has influenced me the most in the way through financial education, is an enterprising businesswoman who has understood very well how the energy of money works and honors its concept, after having lived the maximum profit in salary, then the total bankruptcy, and emerge victorious and improved from this, tells us that the first thing we must understand is that without any doubt, money is energy and we can handle it in our lives as easily as we can block its arrival with our infinite limiting beliefs; also tells us that none of these beliefs are true, thinking that our happiness will depend only on the amount of money we have in our bank account is one of the main blocks to achieving financial success.

"Money is neither good nor bad, money is an amplifier, it is a mean that allows us to make exchanges for the things we want at this moment, whether goods or services."

When we understand the concept of money in this way and remove all negative emotions from money and see it simply as the resource we can use to help many people, it then becomes a very powerful tool.

At this point, we can then say that money is neither good nor bad, but the way we see, handle and use money can be catalogued in this way, according to the consequences and benefits of our actions with respect to our profits. For this reason, Robert Kiyosaki states that one of the correct ways to attract money is to educate ourselves financially, knowing the laws of the place where we are investing or managing a business to understand what advantages we have in front of a demand and also expand the panorama of possibilities and see investments where no one else (or very few) can see them. But the only way to get there is not by working for money, but for the love you put in whatever you do and for what you want to achieve, making mistakes as many times as necessary, and learning everything from sales and marketing to accounting and law.

The world today is in a serious financial crisis because the way our grandparents and parents were educated about money, how to receive it, manage it, and accept it is behind us. The current education system is completely out of date with respect to the new economy and the monitoring of inflation levels. People are still educated only to work, to get a good salary, to buy a house and to support their family, but only those who understand the true value and meaning of money come out ahead because of that, the rich are getting richer and the poor are even poorer, leaving behind the middle class which, depending on how things go, can become extinct at any moment and be "on the side of the rich or on the side of the poor".

Robert Kiyosaki and Donald Trump have noted this worrying situation and in consideration have written a book called "we want you to be rich" to initiate the process of financial education in the citizens of the United States of America and for those who are willing and interested in following the recommendations of this book and live in other countries of the world.

In this book, Robert and Trump comment with concern that the rich who want to improve things only donate money to the causes they believe in. But they in addition to money for foundations and a percentage of the profits from this book for institutions that teach financial education, give their time teaching and educating through their experience.

Trump and Kiyosaki in this book mention that there are three kinds of financial advice: for the poor, for the middle class, and for the rich. The financial advice for the poor is: "that the government will take care of them". The poor have social security and Medicare. The financial advice for the middle class is: get a job, work hard, spend as little as possible, save, invest for the future in investment funds and diversify. Most middle-class people are passive investors: investors who work and invest so as not to lose. The rich are active investors, who work and invest to earn. This book will teach you to be an active investor, to develop your resources to live a wonderful life working and investing to earn.

Knowing this, it is very important that we understand that the only thing that money cannot solve is poverty, simply because of the lack about financial education. Trying to solve our poverty problems with money will only lead to an unhappy, unsatisfied or worse, poor life, because money without financial education does not eliminate poverty.

In order to initiate this transformation of thoughts it is important that we completely forget about deserving, to discard that "I deserve this or that" mentality because I am a high-ranking soldier, teacher, business owner, wage earner or simply poor. The most practical way to solve this problem of poor financial results, distance and low return on money, is to change our way of thinking, start seeing the world and think like rich and not like poor or middle class. Because if we continue waiting for the others with greater capacities and better rank that we take charge, we will obtain again and again the same result, because as a wise man once said "you will never obtain different results as long as you continue to act in the same way". If our view of the world and money does not change, we will eternally be part of a bankrupt society, with well-educated but economically unstable and insecure people.

LOANS, MYTHS AND TRUTHS BEHIND THEM

Albert Einstein once said, "I think it's crazy to keep sending our kids to school without teaching them about money.

Knowledge is power, the importance of studying and knowing financial education today, goes beyond adding, subtracting, multiplying and dividing, knowing accounting and business administration. It is essential to know in a conscious way the work of the numbers, the pros and cons of the debts, the myths and the truths regarding the loans and above all to learn how to generate business strategies that place us in the maximum financial level that is to be investors. As described by Robert Kiyosaki in his quadrant book on money flow. However, all the great businessmen and successful investors emphasize that it is fundamental and of vital importance to study history together with our financial training, because this is the "secret" formula of all the rich people so as not to make the same mistakes of past generations and even help us to foresee the future of all our investments. In addition, knowledge of history can be timely in understanding, interacting and deciding on world events, both politically and financially.

As the saying goes, "Those who do not learn from history are condemned to repeat it.

In the same order of ideas, John Naisbitt in his books, Megatrends, Megatrends 2.0 and 11 Mentalities to foresee the future, tells us about the importance of observation and historical knowledge of the country where we live, of finances, of the great business cases and above all the daily study of each political, social and financial event that surrounds us, because this is what will allow us to program our brain and train us to know the future events and thus be able to foresee and even save all our investments, and if it is the case, our own company.

John, in 11 Mentalities for Anticipating the Future, defines mentalities as:

"Mentalities are key principles or ideas that operate as fixed stars. Our mind is like a drifting ship lost in an ocean of information and clinging to fixed stars we orient ourselves. It is the mentalities that maintain our course and guide us so that we can arrive safely at our destination. A common purpose of the eleven mentalities presented in this book is not to get lost in that which is not essential, but instead to concentrate on the things that have and will have the most influence in our lives.

Therefore, it can be said that a trained mind is a mind that looks for opportunities and does not look for solutions to problems, because it knows that in every opportunity there is an implicit problem that it is capable of solving. But now, what about people who don't study at all about finance and history, and don't train their brains for business and looking for opportunities? Simple, they get into debt. These people tend to always resort to their credit cards for unnecessary expenses, they buy liabilities with financing (which generates even more debts and losses by very high interests), they tend to work too much and they do not see the yield of their money because everything they produce goes in payments at the end of the month, plus the interests and the ants expenses; in addition to that the investments that they make with bank money tend to be "wrong" due to the lack of knowledge on how to multiply the money and to make that this works for them and not on the contrary. A seemingly adequate investment may be the purchase of a house, but what many do not know is that a house (with no lease opportunities or economic advantage) becomes a strong and extremely prolonged liability.

Although it is important to know that none of this is as alarming as it seems, we must consider the need (using this term in a slightly aggressive and categorical way) to have all the correct and exact information regarding the percentages of interest, loans, the credit bureau and of course the good and bad debts.

For this reason, it is important to begin to educate ourselves on all of the above issues, starting by denying some of those "truths" we hear in the street from inexperienced people (even from the same banks and financiers) regarding bank loans and debts.

We almost always make the mistake of listening to advice about financial care and investments, people have not achieved great things in their lives, or yet, they have not achieved "anything" at the financial level, and even, we usually listen to people of apparent success only by their constant flow of money without first asking ourselves if that space in which they are, is the place we want to reach. Among the things they usually tell us (and in many cases, unfortunately we often listen) these would be the most common:

- Bank loans are bad because you have to pay a lot of interest at a high price.

- All the interest, be it from a bank loan or financing in another entity, is too high and you will never be able to pay it off.

- The shorter the financing plan, the better because you won't lose money. It is important to clarify that all financing generates interest so it can be seen as a loss of money depending on the investment. Time has nothing to do with this, because the importance of what has been acquired and the profits it will generate generates greater weight.

- It's best to invest in a home of your own and pay off the credit as you can. This advice may be good depending on the level of inflation where we are, but if it is in a stable or moderately stable economy, it does not apply.

24

- No matter what you buy or if it is going to work for you, when you see that you can acquire it through financing or installments, do it, it will always be a good investment.

- The banks are the worst, if you don't pay the bank fees on time, you will fall into something they call the credit bureau and you will be completely banned from all the credits you want to opt for.

- Watch out for the credit bureau, that's part of the government and they know all about you!

- If you don't pay on time you will be seized and everything you have will be taken away until you are left on the street.

To quote John again to confirm all these previous points and the importance of knowing who to listen to and who not to listen, we must remember that: *"The things that we expect to happen always happen more slowly", which means* that if you hear these kinds of things and also follow them and believe them vehemently, they will end up happening in the same way. Although for the avoidance of doubt and misinformation it is better to continue reading because we will talk about the 7 myths of loans, we will explain what the credit bureau really is and even more we will talk about the two types of debt and when to acquire them.

It is understandable that we are terrified by the idea of getting into debt and thinking about going so far as not being able to make payments, as well as remembering our parents talking about the importance of saving, moderation and discipline. These are the necessary tools for professional improvement and for overcoming any unforeseen event in our daily lives. However, it is understandable that the country's economic situation, the high costs of daily living and unforeseen emergencies sometimes force us to look towards a path known as "the loan".

Now, to eliminate those fears and learn more about these credit issues and make better decisions in the future, let's start with the myths.

Myth 1: **The credit bureau belongs to the government and registers all debtors.**

The reality is that although the credit bureau shares our information with the banks, it is simply a private company that has nothing to do with the government and only handles accurate and concrete information of all people who have ever received a bank credit, which does not mean being on a blacklist, so the bureau is just a company that contains our banking data.

Myth 2: **If you're in the bureau, you can't get any credit.**

FALSE. This does not necessarily mean being exonerated from any credit just for having our banking and payment history, our credit information remains in the bureau database for 6 years. It is important to know that from the first moment we pay the credit, our names and financial behavior are completely recorded, because the bureau updates our information every 10 days and with this data the banks decide whether to grant us credit or not.

Myth 3: Paying for minimum payments will always be the best way

This really is one of the most common myths and greatest compliments of financial history; this is a bad financial habit because although in some cases it can be a great option (according to the business we are doing, the interest and the inflation rate), in other occasions it can be a "knife for our throat", since the profit trick is in the interests. Which means: the longer we take to pay, the more profit the bank will make.

Myth 4: Personal Loans are Extra Income

This is also false. A personal loan is a debt that must be repaid. This is the same mistake that is made when believing that credit cards are for enjoyment. All credits bear interest and are therefore responsible for payments. It is important to remember that all credits generate profits through interest.

Myth 5: Borrowing from friends or acquaintances is better than borrowing from the bank.

This is the main myth that we must remove from our head, first of all because it can bring us many family and financial problems. In addition, borrowing from our acquaintances may seem advantageous, but it really is if the amount is very low and we commit to pay on a timely date for both parties, allowing this to be short term or to one no longer than 3 months..

It is preferable that if we require a much larger loan, we apply to banks, cooperatives or other financial institutions, analyzing of course which offers us the best forms of payment and lower interest rates. If we don't have an income that generates a good ability to pay, then the best thing is not to get into debt because we could put all our reputation at risk and lose relationships with friends and family.

It is important to point out that the only advantage of borrowing from people close to you is that this loan, even if it is short term, may not result in interest losses. However, the best advice is simply not to get this type of loans - debts.

Myth 6: Any credit we get is because we can afford it.

This may be true and at the same time it may not be true, in fact it is a relative myth; indeed the entity makes a credit evaluation of our banking profile and history and verifies if we have the capacity to pay enough to charge us for the financial responsibility we are about to acquire, but this does not mean a guarantee of payment or loan.

Many economists suggest that when we want to get into debt, consider if this loan can be worth it, that is to say that it is a good debt, of those that are taken as an investment that generates great benefits in the future. and that although they offer us more than we have asked for. To do this, we must consider our current situation and be honest about whether or not we will be able to acquire such a debt. It is good to remember that the less we get into debt and the less time we make payments, the better for our pockets and our peace of mind.

Myth 7: If you don't pay, your house will be taken away and collectors will not stop calling you.

It is true that all finance companies have a collection office, and that their function is to be persistent at the time of collection, so much so that sometimes they can get to the point of falling into harassment. However, there are specialized entities that are responsible for publishing the guidelines of conduct for the collection departments of companies and thus prevent them from making calls at inappropriate times or take actions that invade our privacy.

Although it's good to know that the best way to avoid debt collectors is to pay on time and keep all our credit payments current. Besides, this exonerates us from losing what we've mortgaged.

At this point it is good to mention the myth about shipments. Normally we tend to fall into this myth for lack of knowledge. No one can take our home or any other property without us having put it as a guarantee, unless we have acquired a mortgage loan. But usually the companies that grant personal loans ask for a guarantee or a guarantee that depending on the moment can be from a telephone, a tv or any electrical appliance, to a house or a car.

On the other hand, there are some financial entities that can offer you the credits without the need to present a guarantee, simply because we have a good credit history.

It should be noted that there are companies that do not ask for any kind of collateral and usually make personal loans with much lower interest rates compared to the rest. This is the case of some companies that lend money through the web, that is to say, that the personal credits are by Internet and in exchange you only have to have a good financial history.

In the same order of ideas, knowing these myths about loans, understanding the meaning of money and cutting with so many taboos, it is important to consider some recommendations on the subject already exposed.

Recommendations

- Putting together a budget of fixed monthly spending and secure cash inflows will help us keep our accounts in order and know how much money we can and can't count on daily. In order to keep this budget the first step is to know what is the amount of fixed monthly money we receive, then, the best thing we can do is to domicile the payments of services such as electricity, water telephone, among others, directly to our, knowing what is the minimum monthly overhead of services, but calculating it to the maximum to foresee and not have loss of money or negative numbers at the time of drawing accounts.

- Another important recommendation for not acquiring more unpayable debts is not to fill us with interests that exceed (between the sum of all) more than 30% of our monthly earnings, because only in this way will you be able to take a better control of the surplus of money for necessary basic expenses.

- Forget about the ant expenses, those that take away our money for unnecessary and capricious purchases, that look small in amounts but at the end of the month they add a considerable number for effects of our expenses and our savings.

- Last but not least, remember to prioritize your debts and fixed expenses and forget about the idea that credit cards are cash because they don't, they generate interest debts and add information to your credit history.

Very well, now that we know all these myths, we can be more aware when acquiring a bank loan or debt, but before assuming the position of financial leaders and completely refusing to assume any debt (because this position is also valid and very accurate) we must know the difference between a good debt and a bad debt.

When does it make sense to get into debt?

If our goal is to achieve financial freedom, it is important to know that there are debts that will help to achieve that goal and others that will definitely keep us away from it. If you continue to read with enthusiasm, it's because this topic is definitely for you. In this section we'll look at what all this is about good debts, something we've thought doesn't exist and probably just read in this book.

When we talk about debts we can distinguish two types, good debts and bad debts, knowing how to recognize them will make us richer, but if we are not yet able to identify the differences between the two, we can dangerously get stuck for a long time in the rat's career, we and our constant flow of money will go from profits and positive interests, to the misleading state of the rat's career, a term that Robert Kiyosaki explains and defines as the state in which we work only to get out of debt and get more and more credit. This will make us fall into an eternal cycle of collecting - paying - acquiring new debt, making it much more difficult to achieve the financial freedom we so long for.

Now, if our goal is not to reach the life of the much mentioned Robert Kiyosaki and Donald Trump, life with financial freedom, but the reach of static capital (investment in saleable movable goods such as televisions, appliances, sofa games, sound equipment, among others) this cycle or this race of the rat may be an option or a valid game to achieve that goal.

At this point you will surely ask yourself, then what are the good debts and the bad debts? Well, bad debts are all those that we acquire and that can only benefit a bank or anyone who has been the entity that granted us the loan and that in our personal balance (that we have done previously to know our inputs and outputs) becomes a liability that constantly generates expenses and very high interest to pay (more than 30% of our fixed monthly income). Therefore, they become an expense that will come directly out of your pocket and that can only be paid by you with your fixed monthly income, and not with the gain received from the credit acquired.

A classic example of a bad debt is acquiring a good or a service from something we don't really need and which only responds to a whim or impulse of the moment, such as a new refrigerator or a larger television, even though the one we already have still works, or a three-week vacation for which we will be forced to pay very high interests for more than three months.

The fact of acquiring a bad debt, can reflect the lack of control and discipline that we have with our finances, in addition to little knowledge in financial education; these debts usually we acquire them in an unintelligent way and with very dangerous credit instruments such as lenders, credit cards, long-term financing, among others.

But on the other hand, there is the little-known world, or rather, only known to successful people, that is, those with education and financial intelligence; and it is the world or the reality of what they define as "good debts". These are all those debts that we acquire to generate assets that in turn generate even more assets, but this is only possible when we get into debt intelligently. That is to say, that we acquire active goods that generate a financial retribution, or more concretely, they produce money for us; as it can be the acquisition of a commercial premises, a property that generates profits for us (real estate that we can rent), a superior formation (because to educate us financially and of correct form will always be a good investment) or acquiring an antiquity that is revalued with the time by its historical importance. For this last point it is important to know about history in order to avoid acquiring products badly called antiques, which instead of being revalued suffer depreciation, that is to say, they lose their economic value.

A very clear example, given by Robert Kiyosaki, is investment in real estate. If a bank offers us a credit of $500,000, we can take that credit and with the choice of two options, we could get the purchase of a property at $100,000 or less, the remaining money returned to the bank as immediate payment of the credit, this property put it into rent which can be an approximate of $1200 less taxes, and with this rent pay the outstanding installments of the remaining credit. Surely we will obtain a remaining profit of about 200$ net, 200 with which we do not count monthly as a constant income.

On the other hand, with the credit we could buy 5 properties of 100.000$ and rent them; the quotas of the credit would be approximately of 5000$ monthly, if each lease produces us an income of 1200$ deducting taxes, we will obtain 6000$ net, with which we will be able to pay the monthly quota of the bank and in addition we would have an asset of 1000$ monthly that increases when finishing paying the credit. Precisely this is what is known as intelligently managing money, acquiring good debts, generating constant assets and definitely making money work for us, but we can only see this as an investment opportunity when we have financial intelligence.

HOW TO GET OUT OF DEBT AND START EARNING

If you want to stop being poor and start living a rich and millionaire life, without being a victim of global changes, it is important that you develop the most important thing you have with you, YOUR MIND, because your financial education is the main engine for your economic growth.

Remember that the winners have high aspirations, enthusiasm and short, medium and long term plans. Perhaps your ideas may seem out of touch with reality, but it all starts with a dream and a crazy idea, just pay attention to the details and concentrate on seeing which can lead you to make your dreams come true. Donald Trump said one day at a meeting with important businessmen: "I invest to win, don't you?" and only those who had a real financial education felt identified with this, because only winners invest to win, others invest not to lose.

The great business leaders and investors, recommend people who want to live like them, begin to assume successful and be very stubborn to the point of achieving all the objectives. Positive thinking and constancy work and have a lot of power, being a winner requires that kind of power, whether you are extrovert or introverted because shyness here has little to do with it.

Ignorance is very costly, much more so than education, and that includes financial education. The fear of the unknown often causes us to lose millionaire opportunities, do not allow that to steal your aspirations and financial well-being preventing you from achieving the life of the great ones. Power over our emotions and thoughts is one of our greatest strengths and is an important key to success. Being positive and focusing on your financial education can help you overcome difficult situations and determine those people who just want you to feel unable to take advantage of you.

Learn about money, make mistakes, educate yourself and work harder every day until you get the money to work for you, that's the key to successful investments.

Well, now that we have various insights into the key concepts of how the energy of money works, how we can handle it intelligently and what the steps to follow and the way of thinking of a winner are, it is important to also understand how we can get out of our debts quickly and without more complication than generating a good plan of action.

The best way to start is without a doubt, creating the habit of keeping a monthly balance of all our income and expenses, this will allow us to understand more accurately what we are spending our money on and how we are managing it, if it is good or if we are really wasting it. This is important because many times we are not aware of why we get into debt, what we spend the money on or what we invest it in, and many times we do not know if it is really necessary for our financial growth that investment or expense we are thinking of making and we end up with an immense list of all the accounts payable that in time will only generate a great headache, frustration and even much disillusionment and demotivation.

For all this there is a simple solution, if we begin to create the habit of analyzing our expenses in detail, we will be able to know with greater clarity which are really important and necessary and which are not, in such a way we will be much more intelligent at the moment of acquiring our debts and from the first instant we will generate our action plan to leave them as soon as possible and without any type of complications.

There are various exercises and ways to keep our financial control, this practical exercise that you will read below, will offer you a method that consists of only four simple steps to get out easily and quickly of all the debts you may have and will allow you to have absolute control of your money and even the awareness of spending (in what to spend and what not to do) that few have.

STEP 1

IDENTIFY WHERE YOU ARE RIGHT NOW

The first step is as simple as identifying where you are, a question that seems to be very simple but takes an important and profound work of analysis and internalization.

Where are you today? It is of the utmost importance that we respond clearly and honestly to where we are financially at the moment, because this is what will push us to where we would like to be, and in turn will allow us to be clear about what we must do to get there. It is therefore a matter of vital importance.

Sitting down, calculating and getting the total figure of our debt is step 1.1. It is important to clarify that after knowing this sum and see if we have or not the money to get out of it soon is something that can generate a lot of stress, but it is necessary that you take this first step as the beginning to reach the trip of your dreams, or better still to reach your financial tranquility. In the end this process will become a positive consequence of having performed this exercise.

All this is necessary because in order to know how to get out of all our debts, the first thing we must do is make an inventory of how much money we owe, to whom and the reason why we owe it, that is, what we spend it on.

To do this, we will make a table of several columns in an Excel or Word file or in a notebook that we will use to control our finances, and we will classify them in the following way:

First column identifies who you owe (name of subject or store).

Second column, what is the total sum of the debt to each name or invoice mentioned above, if there are several invoices specify them and add them all, and then place the final amount obtained (it is important to place the items on which we spent that money).

Third column, place what is the total sum of interest generated by debts (this is debts with interest such as loans or credit cards, bank loans, financed purchases, etc.).

Fourth column, establishes a minimum monthly payment and if you owe to friends or colleagues, establishes a payment quota to each one proposing them to return their money even if it is in parts. Add up all these payments and establish your total minimum monthly payment, to propose this goal to you on a monthly basis and take it out of the money you have available for food and other expenses. If, on the other hand, you receive money fortnightly or weekly, you can adapt those minimum payments to weeks or fortnights so that you can get out of these debts even faster.

STEP 2

USE THE "SNOWBALL DEBT METHOD"

The snowball debt method is a strategy proposed by Dave Ramsey, author of "The Total Transformation of Your Money", and is performed to eliminate personal debts that we have acquired through credit cards, mortgages and others; this method basically consists of paying first the lowest debt, and making minimum payments to the other larger debts. So, once you have paid that first debt (the smallest and least expensive), you will concentrate on the next smaller debt, and so on until you reach the largest or even total payment of all.

According to Dave Ramsey, this strategy is used in the following way: if, for example you have a $100,000 mortgage, you have an additional $15,000 personal loan, you also have 1.200 dollars of expenses on one credit card and $500 of expenses on another credit card and, besides you have expenses of a receipt or two pending of about $100 in the library or gym or some classes that you take, then you should concentrate on paying off first that debt of $100, also making minimum payment contributions to the rest of your debts (the minimum payment for debts and in general that you determined in step 1). After you have paid off this first debt in full, you should concentrate on paying off the next smaller debt, in this case, the $500 you have on one of your credit cards.

Some accountants and economists think that this system goes totally against financial logic, because any of them will tell you to pay first, and as soon as possible, that debt that regardless of whether the amount is high or low, generates or charges you higher interest because "this way the debt will grow less over time and you can use your money more efficiently". Although this is true in some way and may work, this snowball method doesn't tell you to stop paying the minimum of other debts, for this reason it makes it efficient because what is really behind the strategy has very little to do with efficiency and much more to do with some psychological principles that modify human behavior. This is why the snowball tends to work better than any other strategy for many people.

Why is that? I don't know. Very simply, by paying first or setting aside every penny of dollar you have available to face the smallest debt or lower cost, you can cross that amount relatively quickly from your list of debts, thus becoming more effective to pay the next debt that will be the next lower figure and thus, to get those quick small victories your motivation will increase. This is very important because if you worry too much (to the point of stress and emotional chaos) about the amount of money to be paid and focus first on the largest debts, it will be much easier for you to feel powerless in the face of the large amount of accumulated debt. But by facing the smallest debts until you eliminate them soon from your list, you will begin to win the battle and you will realize that you are capable of winning this financial war.

So, this strategy works the motivation, allowing to see that from the economic organization and establishing a margin of weekly, monthly or fortnightly expenses, you will be able to put an end to that list of accounts payable. It is often better to follow human nature than certain numerical logics (even if they work), but of course this method works better with certain types of people. As any other psychological and cognitive method works, although it will never be too much to know other alternatives.

Don't feel overwhelmed when you take out the structure of steps 1 and 2, this process is very similar to any other that can be spent in an environment of personal productivity to the point where you can get to the point where the mountain called "debts" (too many tasks and projects pending completion) is so overwhelming that you may feel lost, unfocused or hopeless.

So, in that case, it's possible that the snowball approach can help you find the motivation you need to get everything back in order. Don't forget that every time you pay and you have already solved your obligatory daily affairs, you dedicate yourself then to face that small task owed and you begin to cross out, cross out and cross out all the negative numbers that were already paid.

Remember to start from the smallest, because if you're faced with a giant and a little intimidating task you'll probably be scared, but if you reduce the size of the problem and make it small enough, you'll be able to win battles faster and faster. And so, once you've taken full control of your financial life, you'll feel motivated enough to start thinking with a different mathematical logic and much more careful and optimal. In this way it will be easy for you to face any economic decision, to act with efficiency and common sense.

Tatiana Arias and many other people have used this method and have validated it, after having seen good results, and recommend another plus for this strategy that can also work and is that once you have paid the smaller debts, then put the focus on paying that debt that generates higher interest, since that will now be the one that frees you more money when you pay it month after month. But in addition to choosing it and focusing on it, the advice is to pay a little more over the minimum payment whether it's $5, $10 or the amount of dollars that is within your range of possibilities and that eventually does not leave you short at the end of the month to pay other fixed monthly expenses.

Almost always in finance the habit is more important than the amount, that is why, in these cases debtors, if you want to get out as soon as possible from the accounts payable, it is extremely important to enter into a dynamic of paying a little more than the minimum each month.

There are still two more steps to go, but only by consistently applying these first two steps can I assure you that you will be able to get out of your debts very quickly and intelligently.

Remember that your attitude will depend on your motivation to follow the plan, and that only we have the ability to make this task easier and simpler if we have a mentality of focus, perseverance, positivism and of course courage and willingness to win.

ROCKY POWER

Although it may not seem like it, this is one of the most important steps to get out of debt, since it is the one that will keep us focused on our goal, to leave the red numbers at zero.

Those who have seen Rocky's film may remember that some of the things that characterized this character were his perseverance and tenacity to achieve his goal, which was simply to go out to win, for this reason this step is called so, because like him we must take care of our attitude to the circumstances. Since, in order of accounts, it will be this one that determines the time that we will take to pay our debts according to the dates and goals that we set ourselves.

It is important to stop doubting our mind and ability to achieve things, because the right attitude of approach is what will lead us to understand how the energy of money works, how to stay free of debt and make peace with it, to begin to intelligently invest our capital.

STEP 4

POSITIVE MONEY

In this step is where we find the magic that will allow us to get out of debt without the need to earn more money than we already earned; of course, if you get the opportunity to increase your income is also good and important, but remember to start spending your money wisely because the more you earn, the more you spend.

The "positive money" step is a system of "financial happiness" created by Tatiana Arias, this system is based on working the abundance and all that money that is released or created to be available at the end of the month.

And how is that done? Well very simple, the first step to apply this method and get out of debt faster, is through the optimization of monthly fees for basic fixed monthly services such as cell phone, television, electricity, food purchases, among others.

It is important for you to be aware of several things such as: How many technological devices do you have in your home and office that you don't use and don't sell? All of that, instead of having him paralyzed there, can contribute to generating positive money for you.

Many times it is difficult to see this kind of thing as something that can bring us more money, because almost always we tend to feel attachment to these materials that came into our lives through much work effort and surely the first thing that comes to mind when you have to get out of debt is to believe that it is only possible if you earn much more money, and that really is not the case.

If you don't start changing your mentality or habits first, the moment you start earning more money, you'll also start spending a lot more and acquiring materially delinquent and leisure products that will generate more debt. That's why investing your time in trying to change your relationship with money is essential to start your journey and get out of debt, additionally it is just as important that you invest time in working the material detachment, getting to see that objects around you that you can sell because they have a lot of time without use and that their sale will also free you from a few debts and red figures on your list.

Once you change your relationship with money and consistently generate positive money, continually attracting money to you and now thinking much more intelligently financially, then it's time to start investing and making the money work for you and not you for it. Your job at that time will not be to think about how to pay debts when you earn more money, but on the contrary your mission will be to think with the money you earn TODAY, how you will organize your personal finances to begin to pay those debts of acquired liabilities and assume now good debts that generate assets.

Now that you know all the steps and your mind has greater financial education and winning investor mentality, remember to write your own script, that one where you draw your perfect life, then reproduce it and live as you want to do because that is freedom, that is power and that is definitely winning. Grant yourself the dream come true of financial freedom that will lead you to be who you really want to be and work just for the love of what you do and not for the need to generate maintenance money.

Take care, your mind is your most important asset and the main lever to take you to the place where you want to be, then you must be very careful and jealous with what you put it, with what you consume; because sometimes it is much more difficult to get rid of old thoughts and ideas that are already in our psyche than to learn something new and important.

Those cases of "luck" called in some cultures "leverage" can come in many forms, one of them can be your thought. All the successful people that exist in the world take care of their body in an intelligent way and above all they take care of their brain, not only through food but through thoughts, because they do not think about things like "I will never be able to do that", "this is too much for me" "I do not have the necessary money to achieve it" but on the contrary they program themselves looking for solutions and filling themselves with strategic thoughts like "How can I achieve it and what should I do? How can I face those risks and reduce them? How do I get the money I need?

It is important to be clear that life is full of risks and we don't have absolute control of all the things that can happen to us, no matter how much we like to think otherwise. But we do have the capacity to reduce risks and increase our growth and financial freedom through learning, the reasonable and reasoned decisions we make and, of course, our positive and persevering attitude towards situations. Many financially successful people like Donald Trump have achieved that freedom even though all odds were against them and they did it because they decided to take control of their destiny and refused to give up so easily.

Robert Kiyosaki and Donald Trump say, "*If you do the minimum, you'll get the minimum. In the end, your results won't be exceptional. To stand out, you must do what others are not willing to do.* You can make the most of your time and all the talents and potential you have and the place where you are now and where you want to go. You just have to get ready to do more. What you're willing to do is what determines how far you're going to go.

That's why it's important to control not only our income and expenses, and keep our debts badly paid, but also to educate yourself; for the more you learn, the more you'll realize how much you didn't know and the less time and business opportunities will go unnoticed in front of you.

The best and most important thing to achieve our financial freedom is that we learn to think for ourselves through constant financial education, trial and error, and perseverance, until we polish our own eagle's eye, rather than someone else who might not have good intentions doing it for us. Taking courses in accounting and business law is important for those who want to manage money intelligently and invest it to put it to work for themselves, no matter they do not have the plan to be accountants or lawyers, this will save them several years of "mistakes".

As Louis Pasteur said, "Chance favors prepared minds." But if, on the other hand, your goal is just to stay debt free and lead a quiet, uncomplicated life is fine, it's important as an adult to know what lifestyle you want. No one is good or bad, the question is that you start planning now what you want and materialize it before it is too late, especially if the main desire is to live like Queen Elizabeth and her relatives, then the suggestion is to start looking for that castle right now.

Life is too short not to dream of achieving that castle, or whatever aspect keeps for you your dream and need, but it is important not to forget that there are more important things than money, start investing in that which you love because love is the key to a life of health, wealth and happiness. It is much easier to be healthy if you are happy, it is much easier to be rich if you are happy and it is even easier to be happy if you love what you do.

How to be Debt Free: Volume 2

A Proven Strategy to Take Control of Your Financial Freedom by Getting Rid of Debt, Loans, Student Loans Repayment, Credit Card Debt, Mortgages and More

By

Income Mastery

Introduction

In this life, we get into debt for acquiring things, let's start there. Whether it's to pay for our children's school, open our first business, buy a car, buy a house or improve the one we already have, and so on. However, without emotional intelligence we are not doing well in financial life. It is not bad to have debts, that we will repeat perhaps more than once through the book. The bad thing is to let ourselves be carried away by false expectations of stability, not knowing how much we have in our pockets and with the perhaps indiscriminate use of the credit card, not only do we acquire things, also debts, interests, and scores for or against the various entities. The disastrous consequences would be the seizure of present and future assets, not accessing any more credit and, consequently, continuing to owe our creditors.

As a person who already generates income and expenses, I consider that some episodes of my life and also those of people around me, are necessary and important to learn how to organize ourselves, not only at work and personally, but also in terms of finances. In this edition you will see the different types of credits to which we have access, the unfavorable complications for us, the abuse of the mentioned credits that could become almost unpayable debts, and yes, I tell you almost because no entity is going to want to lose a client, no matter how delinquent the coordination with the different financial and banking entities to be able to pay the debt in installments.

Also, as people we must understand that no matter how small, you should not use money that is not from one to pay other debts that we have, although there are exceptions that being used wisely, would generate income. And it's just one of the cases we're going to review.

I will repeat: Having debts is advantageous, one of them is that it can be the origin to start that enterprise that you still have in mind but that you did not find the way to start. Here we'll introduce you to him.

Did you know that you are buying investment and spending at the same time on a car? Of course, because when you give it the use you want, it already begins to lose its value in the market, and in a short time you will have to replace or sell it to recover something invested.

I have another apprenticeship for you: You are one day at work and can quietly have a coffee, eat a snack, have lunch outside the office, buy another snack, drink another drink, you have the audacity to pay for it with the attractive and dangerous "plastic money" when you realize, at the end of the month, that you have to pay off a good amount of ant debt that you could have avoided.

And as well as the ant debt, you can also acquire debts to be able to arrive with tranquility at the end of the month. I remind you, and excuse me beforehand how bad there might be in the next sentence, but a staff cut and no savings to face an undesirable unemployment, and you grab your head to blame yourself "'Why didn't I foresee this situation?'".

Although there are some concepts of debt below, remember that a well-managed debt is a debt in our favor.

Do you remember I told you that banks are interested in not losing us as customers? Sure, and one of its ways is to buy our debt, what we have to coordinate with the bank is if you can provide us with payment dates in our favor.

This and other lessons we will learn through the book, with illustrated examples, and in you is how to apply the different alternatives of solution that are presented to you.

One of my favorite methods of generating savings is the 50-30-20 Do you know it. And if you know him, did you use him in your own finances? That's having control of your money in your hands, knowing that part of your money will not go into debt ants, but for the opening of new horizons.

It reminds me of the situation of a career colleague: He was in a job for a regular time. He had already made his savings but what he did not foresee was that the job search would take him two years, in which he had had various forms of income but did not receive what he earned in a more established work environment regulated by labor law, and much of what he had saved diminished considerably. But he also invested it in his complementary education to the studied career, guaranteed that this money returns in the form of a better labor situation. And that happened. It has been more than a year and a half since this colleague has been working in the agency in which he is. He was able to raise more money again and with a bank loan, first he rented, and then he bought an apartment.

We seek our improvement, seeking how to intelligently get out of the debts that invade us. There are methods that I do not recommend using, however it is there in case the financial situation is already unsustainable.

I would also like to bring up another example of perseverance and saving to come out of a situation that could manage a debt: A time when I worked in a startup agency, two of my colleagues were the best at creating content. They came to earn enough and be quoted to other agencies. However, when the statistics of a certain social network changed, they had to be dismissed. One of them emigrated to the newsrooms and goes on a trip when her vacations come up, this is once a year; the other, with the savings she had, strengthened and consolidated herself as a content creator, has an income that generates a clothing sales venture, and also travels when she pleases. He was able to put together a good entrepreneurial team that generates income for him and he continues to work on them, from the comfort of his own home.

I hope I have encouraged you with this introduction to what this book is really about and discover how to overcome your debts.

Chapter 1 - Debts, Vehicle Loans, Student Loans, Mortgages, and More

In memory of a beloved journalism teacher, I'll begin with his familiar opening phrase of class. Debts to pay, debts to schedule, debt purchases, loans to buy cars, master's degrees, doctorates, your home or dream space ... so many elements. But before we start, let's make a quick diagnosis of the situation:

- To pay, you borrow from another side.

- You can only cover the minimum payment on your credit cards.

- You use 'plastic money' for payments you used to make in cash.

- You run out of money in the middle of a fortnight and the rest you finance with cards.

If you feel identified, alert. For those who still doubt the phrases, let's say that if you don't have enough capital to pay your monthly bills and save at least 10% each month, something is wrong, maybe you are living above your means, as Roberto Bello describes it.

What does it mean to be in debt?

By debt we mean a commitment or obligation entered into in relation to someone or something to replace a situation. The definition of debt is mostly applied in contexts where there is some economic activity. It's worth saying: business, buying and selling, loans, and more.

There are 4 types of debts:

Ant debt:

It is given by the lack of administration in their finances. These are small payments and expenses that cause you to incur in loans and credit. Examples: using cards to buy your daily items, borrowing money from friends, or spending before you receive your season ticket. These small expenses gradually become a snowball effect that at the end of the month, instead of dedicating yourself to saving that part, turns out to be spent, sometimes very foolishly.

Fictional debt:

It's about living beyond our means. What you receive month after month creates an illusion of stability. An example of my own is that I applied for a strong loan when I was working for a newspaper company and thought I could stay a while, so I applied for a two-year car loan. I only kept my job for 8 months and was too tight to pay for the car, so I had to sell it just to cover part of the debt. Don't feel like you're stepping on clouds.

Leverage Debt / Invest:

Leverage is when a person invests money that is not their own, in a business or a proposal, which comes from a credit or loan.

If success is achieved, very well. But if you fail it can mean a big mistake for your personal finances.

I'm going to tell you an example of this type: I worked for a medium time in a content creation agency, which began as a startup, a concept of a newly created company that commercializes products and/or services through the intensive use of information and communication technologies (ICTs). When the business seemed to project well, is where the social networking platform that was used, Facebook, adjusted its algorithms and made the scope of the content go down to levels that paid them little money. Then my boss fired most of the employees and only kept one project, which belonged to his brother, to focus his efforts on getting it through, and I must say it was profitable.

Another example is, a loan that my mother turned her skill into leveraged debt. She had asked for the money to enlarge her marital property, and since we live near a commercial area, i.e. markets, small businesses, street vendors that generate profits, she decided to lend part of the money from the property to these merchants and charge them a friendly interest rate, easier to repay than that of the financial or usual lenders. Of what he had to pay back in 12 months, he was able to get the money back in just two months. Yeah, she projected herself.

A good way to leverage is by buying a property to rent later. The minor debts or mortgage of this property will be paid automatically with the payment of rent. Another example would be to apply for a car loan, buy a car and use it for taxi applications.

This type of debt is the only one that can generate yields and growth.

Subsistence debt:

It is acquired in order to make ends meet. You must meet 2 conditions: The first is to use the money only to pay for basic things: food, housing or health. No luxury or leisure expenses. Generally used by people who have more than one person economically dependent on them, due to the urgency of money at the time, often accept exaggerated interest rates. A real-life example is that a friend and his girlfriend borrowed $200 each month to help his mother, and the interest to pay was very high.

Having debts has its advantages

Yeah, give it to play again. Whenever you think about making an investment that improves your quality of life, it adequately analyzes why you get into debt and that the instalments and interest you will have to pay will be amply rewarded by the benefit you obtain with the good or service for which you get into debt. If you are responsible for your debt and don't spend more than you own, it will suit you well. Consider the following factors when you go into debt to invest:

- Ability to pay

- Contract terms and conditions

- Interest rate

- Methods of payment

- Debt capacity

And these are the advantages of having an investment debt.

- **Increases your credit history** that will help you to be seen positively by various banking and derivative entities at the time of applying for loans or services.

-   **The loan allows you to make investments or take advantage of opportunities** that can generate income over time. One example is a friend, a veterinary student, who asked for a large sum of money to set up a pet shop at home while not attending college. What generated him in pet restrooms, accessory sales and health care, he was able to repay the loan, renew his grooming instruments and pay for an academic semester to go back to school.

-   **Improve your quality of life and your prospects:** Debt responsibly when your quality of life can improve and you don't have time to save is fine. An aunt of mine, after being a nurse, decided with her husband, after using her savings and the loan provided by the bank, to be trained in everything related to telephone technician. He went from educating 10 people in the basement of his house, to having an institution with more than 800 students a month who were educated to be telephone technicians and teleoperators. He improved work, education, family and financially in a relatively short time.

-   **Allows you to organize your cash flow into several future installments**. The money you request can be paid in parts. It only depends on the agreement you make with the person who gives you the loan. I remember making two moves with my credit card: I took out a $250 personal loan and bought a cell phone for about $300. And I had both debts on a par because I was able to arrange for her to make ends meet with the income she received.

- **A well-managed debt can be the beginning of an entrepreneurial life.** This capital will help you get those first few months of your business up and running. I still remember the first days of my parents' business, in which from a small hairdresser, he grew up in a bazaar and bookstore, in 3 years.

- **The loan helps in an emergency:** Because it can allow you a better way out of the situation that you or your family face. It happened in my family life: Several years ago, my family lived in a small apartment with a narrow entrance alley. One day, my then 7-year-old brother was playing with our mascot, a mongrel dog, in the alley and near them a glass bottle. As the two bounced off the bottle, it broke, and a splinter cut off part of my brother's face. My parents used the credit card to pay for the health emergency, including cosmetic surgery.

Did you know that your debt can be good or bad...or very bad?

Yes, it had been warned before that there is no good or bad debt, but debt in our favour. But it's not wrong for you to guide you so you can make a decision about the situation your debt is in.

Good debt:

It is still a debt, with an added value for us, such as, for example, getting into debt for the purchase of a home, as the property will possibly increase its value in the future. And I can assure you, yes. My young father bought an undeveloped piece of land for $6,000. He made a couple of floor and entrance arrangements, sold it to someone else for $13,000, and in 4 years, the new owner sold it to the current owner of the place, who is selling it for $40000 as of the day I write these lines.

Another example is the payment of some studies, because they serve to acquire knowledge that will help you get a job and earn enough money to solve the debt and improve your quality of life. One more example is the acquisition of a debt to set up a business. Of course, with this you are taking a risk, so if it goes wrong, the concept of "good" debt obviously wouldn't apply. But in the opposite case, in which the profits generated by the business are sufficient to be able to repay the credit and obtain a good return.

The American businessman and writer Robert Kiyosaki states in his book "Rich Father Poor Father": "Good debt is the debt that makes you richer, like a loan for an investment property or for the purchase of equipment for your business that will make you a close return. This is the type of debt that is used to buy assets.

I illustrate an example of life: My father, whose father was from a coastal province, has decided to buy a property on my grandfather's land, the cost of which is the equivalent of $360, and after a good time, its cost will be approximately $1490. A debt today, an investment tomorrow.

In short, good debt has to do with long-term value.

Bad debt:

It is that which is acquired to satisfy a need which is not of vital importance and which, moreover, we cannot afford. They do not generate income and some initial debt increases by adding interest that cannot be absorbed by economic growth.

Examples are the purchase of a good that we do not need and cannot afford, such as a television or a kitchen, or products or services whose repayment terms are longer than the duration of the product financed, such as a trip paid by credit card, are some examples of this type of debt.

An example of bad debt is a cousin of mine, who bought a pool table that becomes a dining table. But after a short time, the table began to present deficiencies such as moths in the furniture, curvature of the smooth surface by humidity, among other problems, so my cousin has to spend on repairs.

Another example of bad debt is that of a friend of mine and his wife, who rented a space overlooking the street from his mother's house to set up a business of copying, bazaar and payment of services. Bad administrative management, and few profits, made the business go bankrupt, but from what has been earned in it, you can pay the debts acquired in the financial.

In short, people use credit to acquire goods that lose value and that generate more expenses than benefits, will generate their bad debt.

Very bad debt:

The worst debts are those that have a very high Annual Percentage Rate (APR): ATM credits, deferred or minimum credit card payments, and quick credits. If you do not control those debts can cause the snowball effect, you will owe more than before because of your lack of control.

To deal with this, consult your budget, calculate how much the additional costs of repaying the loan or credit plus interest will be per month. Ask yourself the following questions:

- Do you need it?

- Do you need it now, or could you wait until you could pay it in cash?

- How much more will it cost you to buy it with credit than if you used cash?

- Can you afford the monthly payments?

- What other things will you have to sacrifice in order to pay the monthly dues?

- What APR do they charge you? Could you get better conditions?

- Are you charged for other expenses not included in the APR?

- How much is the total cost?

- How much will monthly payments go up if interest rates go up?

Yes, I was in very bad debt and I'll tell you how I got to this, so you won't repeat it: In August 2016, I overused the credit card of a well-known bank in my country. Before I continue, I will handle the amounts in American dollars, since the currency in my country is the only new currency but it could cause confusion in you, people who read me. Let's move on. I generated a debt equivalent to $350. Then, I continued to hinder my credit history, paying the minimum amount, which would be about $290 each month, because at that time I was earning about $475 a month. If I paid off my debt in full, I would only have about $85 left to live on that month, and at least $59 a month in transportation. I would no longer be able to afford food, housing or services. At that time, I lived in a room near my workplace, but I had to go out on commissions, and the duration of the consulting was four months, not including bonus payments, medical breaks or other inclusions I could earn as a worker for the company I was in. In December of that year my consulting ended, but I was still paying the minimum of that $290 debt, thanks to another lower income as an advertising validator in an online teleworking company. By the beginning of 2017 I was up to my neck in that debt. Yes, it happened and I narrate it so that no one else repeats my example.

Vehicle loans

A vehicle loan is a loan to acquire a car granted by a bank, savings bank or financial institution. You can have the car immediately and pay for it in up to 60 months, counting on the option of advance payment which is the total cancellation of the debt before what was agreed, of the wildcard quota, which is to stop paying one month and of the deductible insurance, depending on each entity.

Please take vehicular credit with your country's currency, not in dollars, due to inflation in the exchange rate.

Try to find 3 or 4 proposals from different financial institutions. Keep in mind the car we aspire to so that we can make various quotes according to model, year and brand. To the entity that offers the second-best proposal, we can present the proposal given to us by the first entity, and also provide you with the third and fourth best proposals. This promotes competition as well as better credit terms.

I don't know about you, but in my country, Peru, you can sell second-hand cars (I warn you not only second). That yes, many of them are many years old, they break down from time to time and generally the car is used for taxis, they wouldn't enter a taxi app, but they can carry a slightly heavy load. It is explained to the borrower that the amount requested on credit is for the purchase of a second-hand car. It happens the transaction money-auto, and then to the car you begin to make it work of taxi, of personalized taxi, of shared taxi, and even transport of diverse objects.

Some financial institutions offer the so-called "Smart Buy" that offers lower fees, and as long as you continually renew your car. Here's an example: imagine that the car we want to buy is worth $10,000. In a normal credit, assuming an initial of $2,000 (20%), the bank would lend us $8,000 so we could pay them back in up to 60 months. In the Intelligent Buying system, we would be financed 30% ($3,000) in two years or 40% ($4,000) in three years. When the deadline is met you have 2 options: you keep the car and refinance the remaining amount or buy a new car with a new smart purchase.

In case you have a car, it can be used as collateral and being part of a loan, this is called a collateral loan. Your car will not stay with the borrower, because a chip will be installed in your vehicle until you pay off your debt.

Pawnbrokers usually have a contract that can be renewed if you can't pay it back after the period. Keep in mind that when you renew you will have to pay the interest and commissions, and you will have to do it until you can pay the total debt, otherwise the entity that lent you the money will auction off your car to recover the amount it lent you.

The purchase of a car goes from being an investment to an expense, due to the fact that the more mileage, tire disorders, bonnets, and more, the car loses a percentage of its value, which will increase over time. A better example are the cars of the taxi apps, they ask for them to be almost new, because they are already losing their value, a new one will be looked for that replaces the one of the fleets.

If they do not comply with the payment schedule, they start by calling the client repeatedly to notify him of the debt and the possible forms of solution and consequences, then a final warning is made. If the debt is generated by not paying the installments belonging to a personal loan, the entity will apply default interest and additional commissions increasing the amount of money owed, while the financial offers a restructuring to extend the term and reduce the amount of the installments thus facilitating payment. If the nonpayment of the debt persists, the lending institution will initiate the pertinent legal actions that may result in a seizure of the debtor's automobile, present and/or future assets.

Whoever has gone through this situation of not being able to contribute in order to pay for the car and overcome this bitter episode in his life, has my respect.

Student Loans

Student loans are an alternative for someone to enhance their professional development and expand their career opportunities. Keep in mind the additional expenses that are generated due to study such as travel and living expenses, in the case of studying at a foreign university, which could raise the cost of financing, as well as equipment or special tools for studying. Review all the financial options to find educational loans that help finance studies is not complicated at all, so it is suggested not to hire the first one that appears along the way. You can apply for credit even if you are halfway through your career.

A friend of the university, requested scholarship in the state entity to cover part of his studies in Spain and in addition, family contributions, meetings of collaboration of part of our friends as a whole and the student loan that asked for it to certain entity of rural box, could finally complete his trip to take a master in political sciences within 2 years, whose chronogram of payments has been extended to 5 years, counting the first ones of his master's degree.

Public entities dedicated to education, as well as banks, financial institutions and municipal savings banks grant various types of educational loans for study materials, undergraduate, master's and doctoral degrees. Its payment period is 5 years and its amount to lend is the equivalent of US$ 30,000 and advises you with facilities.

Private educational institutions also offer educational loans. An example of what I am talking about are the loans that my private university used to make so that, once the educational career is over, and plus a job at the same university, the educational credit requested would be paid off in a certain time (in this case up to a maximum of 10 years). Of course, some of the conditions that the university requires of the student must be met, such as being in undergraduate studies and being placed in the upper third, as one of the best students in their faculty, in addition to being placed in the medium and high pension scales of the university (scales are pension systems in which the student pays according to his economic situation, in this university there are 9 levels, 1 being the lowest and 9 the highest).

Keep in mind that if your loan cannot be repaid, the bank will attempt to collect your debt directly or through a collection agency, as well as taking legal action. Let's try not to get to that extreme measure.

Mortgages

A contract by which a debtor pledges real estate to the borrower from whom he or she receives the loan amount. Thus, if the debtor does not pay his debt, the creditor may sell the asset to collect the unpaid amount. Houses or land are objects of mortgage, however, also lends for the figure vehicles or works of art. A mortgage contract consists of three key elements as:

-Capital. The amount of money borrowed that will be repaid periodically until the debt is paid in full. Your capital can be $2,000, $5,000, $1,000 or more.

-The **period of time stipulated in** advance in which the payment of the debt must be completed, as well as all the monthly payments that the debtor has to make. When my mother finished making that real estate arrangement, which consisted of the construction and fitting out of two mini apartments, the payment time was set at 3 years.

-The interest rates. Cost of more than the debtor pays the creditor for borrowing that money. It can be fixed or variable, can be reviewed periodically and change the amount to pay. I have been able to read in the media in my country that since the beginning of 2019, the downward trend in interest rates on mortgage loans has remained constant, and one of the reasons is the global context, and a voracious competition from the banks and a greater participation of state programs dedicated to housing.

Observe if your real estate is not correctly registered in the Public Registries, you could see your property rights affected against third parties and those of the entity that granted you the credit because the mortgage will not be able to be registered. In the provinces of my country, certain properties still do not have a title to back them up. You have to be careful with that.

An example is my friend, who signs a mortgage contract with a bank, which becomes the creditor. The contract states that the bank will lend you $50000 (principal) at an annual interest rate of 7%. My friend will repay this loan over a period of 20 years (in monthly installments) leaving as collateral a plot of land valued at $70000.

There are two types of mortgages:

1. **Mortgage loan.** It is closed and due to the fact that it has certain conditions in the contract, in the event of wanting to make any modification such as extending the term and amount to be financed, once the loan is formalized, it must be replaced by another, so that the first one is cancelled.

   Keep in mind that if the mortgage loan on your home or other property has not been paid, the creditor will apply to a judge for foreclosure. You will have another period of about a year to pay off the debt, but if you don't do it this time either, his house will be auctioned off and you will have to abandon it, losing any right as owner. If the house cannot be auctioned off for the full amount owed to the bank, plus expenses, even after losing your home, you will still owe the bank and the bank will be able to demand payment from its guarantors or seize their other assets.

2. **Mortgage credit**. This is that the financial institution grants a certain amount of money and the holder decides to dispose of all or only part of it. Each time you need a pending amount, you can use it, as long as it does not exceed the limit of the credit that was granted to you.

There is also a reverse mortgage, which is a credit or loan secured by a mortgage that falls on the main residence granted once or through periodic benefits, to a person who must be over 65 years old. The bank will give you for the house during your life while you can continue using it. Upon their death and according to the modality chosen, the heirs may choose between returning the money to the borrower and recovering the home or collecting the remainder of the loan.

An example is what the grandfather of a friend of mine did, while he was alive and at 72 years of age, he mortgaged his house and lived on the money given to him by the bank. When the old man died, the children were hesitating between paying their father's mortgage, because it was onerous, or finishing using the money for the mortgage, which was already little left.

There are several types of mortgage credit:

- **Traditional mortgage credit.** These are personal loans to acquire land or real estate, which will then function as a guarantee of payment, through the establishment of a mortgage. My grandfather used this method, mortgaging the house in which he was born, to be able to acquire a house in the capital, he did it to guarantee the payment of the second house.

- **Shared mortgage credit.** It's a collective credit, a group of people share the debt. At the time of the credit evaluation, the applicants' income is added together. A coworker and her husband opted for this type of credit for the acquisition of an apartment in the financial district of the capital. They sustained their income levels, the higher the income, the more likely they were to have money to pay off the credit debt. They presented their current debts, duly paid on the corresponding dates. And his financial history, unerringly.

- **Mortgage credit for construction.** It is provided for the expansion, remodeling, and/or construction of a single-family home. My mother's sister, a housewife, inherited a house from my grandfather, and there was no commercial movement in it, but there were signs of a future rental business: Two shops and an alley for additional business. My aunt applied for this type of credit to improve both the shops inside her property and the rooms she needed in her home. And it turned out to be profitable.

Other types of debt

The other types of debts are those contracted with bank or departmental credit cards, which by using them you already manifest your credit history for the various entities for future loan offers but if not used intelligently, reduces the ability to save money and if financial emergency situations arise, it would be the beginning of our economic misfortune.

Personal debt repayment loans are not good counselors. If you don't have an emergency fund of at least three months to be able to make payment on that credit, consider your credit history with points against it.

Being a guarantor for someone who later becomes delinquent can also carry you into debt.

I repeat and it may sound like a charge with that, but for every debt there is a payment plan according to what you are looking for: Trips, weddings, and other elements that are considered onerous and you need a credit support which will lead to debts.

Chapter 2 Getting Out of All Debts

Take control:

Write down in a notebook dedicated to finance, on one side your income and on the other side write down the expenses by category:

- Transportation: how much you spend on gasoline, repairs, maintenance and insurance.

- Home: Electricity, water, telephone, Internet service, cable TV, gas, maintenance or credit payment.

- Food: make an approximate budget of how much you leave in restaurants (including coffee with friends). If you prepare at home, how much you spend on buying products.

- Recreation: trips to the cinema, theatre, concerts, trips or any other entertainment.

- Health: regular medical check-ups, dentist, purchase of a medication on a regular basis.

- Insurance: life insurance, medical expenses, education for your children.

- Education: school, private classes, courses of interest.

- Payment of debts: what you must pay monthly or more if you can for a special issue, such as receiving your Christmas bonus.

- -Miscellaneous expenses: Place the leaks you have a month, however insignificant they may seem, because these are the ones that make you lose control of your finances such as catalogue purchases, cosmetics, hairdressing, laundry, dry cleaning, visits to the spa, birthday gifts, among others.

Calculate your debt capacity

The general formula is established as follows:

Debt Capacity = (Total Income month - Fixed Expenses month) x 0.35.

Regarding Debt

A credit counselor from any bank, financial institution or municipal savings bank can help you manage the debt or debts and list them, make a budget, as well as make a payment plan or reschedule, which does not affect your credit history, in order to pay off that commitment. Negotiate a fair payment so your debt doesn't increase.

Another option is to **refinance a debt,** it affects your credit history, but you will be able to cancel your debt with a new payment order and it will also change the current amounts. What you're asking for is a little delay in the payment date of your next installment. Since you can't afford it, the interest rate you initially had will stay the same. Besides, it won't change your status in the face of central risk either.

The purchase of debt by banks is an alternative to consider, as this option will allow you to consolidate each of your debts into a single entity. Banks offer you this option if you are a good player, not if you are already at a loss. You will be able to standardize your debts and pay only one credit to an entity, with lower rates. All the banks are queuing up to get your loyalty through it, you'll get calls from them from time to time. Just don't wait too long before you apply.

Check how much you spend on ants like morning coffees, cigars, snacks or outings with friends. You'll have to make some sacrifices to discover your ability to save.

Return credit cards through handling fees:

Driving fees are what the bank charges you for providing you with a credit card. If you have five credit cards you will be paying five handling fees, and that money could be used better. Consider returning credit cards and consider handling fees.

A trick to apply to debt number one (if you have a lot of debts), pay the minimum plus 10% you managed to save with your spending cut. Keep it up until you pay off your first debt in full. Don't suspend the minimum payment on the rest of your debts. It is generally recommended to avoid the minimum payment to the maximum, but it is used in this supposedly because you cannot make a larger payment. When debt one is over, it goes to number two. To this liability you must destine the minimum payment, plus the amount you made for debt one. Repeat this process until you liquidate it. When your debts are paid off, you continue to save 10% of your income and convert the payment accelerator into a permanent savings generator.

Use the 50-30-20 method: 50% of your salary must be spent on basic expenses. The last 30% goes to personal expenses. And 20% of the money you make has to go into saving.

You can also save half of your income whether its salary increases, private work, work incentives, sales of objects in disuse, in case you want to create a long-term fund.

If you owe $100 and you are charged interest of $5 dollars a month, and the only thing you do, month after month, is take the $5 out of your wallet, you will never pay your debt. Capital subscriptions are that extra money you give so that the base, or capital, i.e. the $100 in the example, is reduced and so are the interests.

If you decide to make a capital contribution to your debt with the bank, you have two options:

Either the amount of the payment is reduced, that is, you pay less; or the time of the loan is reduced, which means that you keep paying the same but for less time.

In order to get out of debt, automating your bills each month will make sure to help you reduce the amounts you owe.

Pawn is an easy way to get money because you can turn things you already have into cash, things you already have at home and cover a debt. However, once the pawns are in the hands of the pawn shop, it will be more expensive to recover them and you run the risk of not being able to do so if you do not pay on time. Deadlines vary by pawn shop and depending on the items: Jewels, watches with fine Swiss machinery, cars, bicycles, cameras and video cameras, video game consoles and video games, computer equipment, electronics, mini-components, televisions and screens with the latest trends, Smartphone, kitchen and crockery batteries, household appliances, white goods, living rooms, dining rooms and bedrooms, musical instruments, mechanical and electrical tools and leather goods.

No more credits because it is contradictory, interest and mismanagement of resources can further increase debt. Debts are NOT paid with more debts.

If you have a company account retirement plan in which you work, you can get a company loan of your retirement money. It avoids you to pay additional taxes and penalties, if you are punctual in the payment, because of not paying the loan after a term, then you will have to pay those taxes and penalties. And be careful in case you lose your job, because you would have to pay the loan immediately and pay the taxes for the withdrawal of the money before time.

A life insurance policy will allow you to borrow money from the policy at a very low interest rate to solve your debt problems. You don't have to repay this loan, but life insurance benefits will be reduced by the amount you borrow plus interest.

As a last resort you would choose bankruptcy to solve your debts. Declaring bankruptcy is a temporary relief on your debts, however you create a negative impact on your credit history that will affect future loan applications.

Vehicle loans

If you are going to buy a car, compare the interest rates offered by financial institutions and choose among the best vehicle loans.

It will be necessary for the client to execute an initial delivery that must be between 10% and 40% of the value of the car depending on the selected term and the entity. The disbursement includes the insurance for the automobile and the tax deduction, if possible, try to make that delivery as big as possible to reduce the term and interest established for the credit.

In the case of a pledge loan, the monetary obligations established in the contract with which the vehicle contracted the pledges must be cancelled. As long as the debt is not paid to the company creditor of the pledge, the pledge cannot be lifted.

An ideal is that you pay your installments in three and not five years, because the car has a replacement value. After that time, you sell the car and that money can be used for the down payment and for the remaining balance, again you look for another credit. So, every three years you have a new car and you don't overdo it.

If your vehicle debt is in dollars and your income is in national currency or you are over-indebted, prepaying the debt is a good option, because to lower the exchange rate, buy dollars to prepay the debt.

Another option to consider are collective funds, which are a savings fund through which goods and services are obtained, in this case, a car. A group of people get together and all make scheduled payments on a monthly basis, allowing each of them to access the vehicle they are paying for. When you register, you will have to buy a certificate and the number of quotas will depend on each particular case; once you finish canceling them, you access the vehicle. Please note that the car will not be delivered at the start and you will continue to pay for it. Find out if the model you would like to purchase is available in this mode. You can also dispense with the "I finish paying and take it with me", because if you have a high amount of money, you can finish paying several installments and thus get out of the payment faster. The cost will be lower compared to banks, because you are not paying interest. Collective fund entities ask for fewer requirements than when you apply for a vehicle credit, such as identity card, receipt of services and some document with which income can be credited, such as your last payment slip.

Student Loans

Always choose a monthly amount you can afford. Find out about forgiveness, cancellation, and annulment programs as soon as possible, either within the various entities or educational institutions that provide them. You can also make additional and specify how to apply, in this case to the student loan, what it will do is reduce the amount of interest as well as the total cost of the loan.

Working overtime at the current job and getting a second job with flexible conditions, or having a job online, would help contribute to a decrease in credit. Choose to start an online business and minimize expenses. It's not a good idea to stop paying or file for bankruptcy, because apart from shattering your credit history, your debt will continue to spread.

Mortgage loan

Banks have every intention of renegotiating your mortgage and you, to be assertive with the creditor to get better payment terms. Negotiate:

-Better conditions (novation).

-Transfer the mortgage to another entity (subrogation).

-They are more flexible so you don't get another unpaid mortgage.

Remember that in order to terminate the mortgage, it is not enough that the entire loan has been repaid, but it must be recorded in the Register, since if the mortgage is not made it will continue to appear as "alive". This requires the bank to consent to the cancellation and the costs are borne by the borrower.

Other types of loans:

By taking out a personal loan, you are guaranteeing all of your present and future assets so that in a situation of prolonged non-payment, the entity can get a judge to seize these assets, which include your home, your car, your bank accounts, part of your pension, etc. everything necessary to pay off the debt.

Most chronic debtors directly or indirectly involve family and friends in their debts, but in a harmful way: by asking them to come out as collateral for their loans, by borrowing money directly from them, or by using their resources to get into hidden debt without telling them anything. Involve family and friends in a different way, talk to them and tell them honestly about the level of debt, the legal situation (if any) and other related issues. The only way for the environment to help in this problem is through affective support and understanding. Don't ask any more of them.

You don't assume other people's debts either, no matter how much you want or appreciate them, it's not a positive alternative for your pocket. I explain it to you this way: You have an acquaintance who has just made a commitment to the bank or financial institution, which requires a guarantor.

To your surprise you are the chosen person, so you have to know that if that acquaintance cannot assume the payment, you will have to face it. The moment that person stops paying their debt it becomes your responsibility. And in this case, if you're just struggling with learning how to get out of debt, imagine how it affects you to have to pay someone else's debts.

Credit cards or signature loans should be eliminated directly from your day to day. I recommend leaving the plastics "resting" in some drawer of the house and not to carry them, to avoid the temptations.

Elaborate an austerity plan: Say goodbye to street coffee, the taxi, meals outside and all those "ant debts" must be eliminated until the debt stream has decreased. It takes willpower to resist spending.

Generate extra income with the passive income that will come after renting part or all of the place you live. Monetize your hobbies. There are people who their love of photography, videos and narratives, end up making business out of it. You get paid for what you like.

You could always pay the debt with a higher interest rate, in the traditional way, because you end up with the debts that cause you higher interest rates, reducing your final cost.

Another method known as snowballing will require these steps to pay off debts.

3. Order your debts from lowest to highest amount of money in debt.

4. Make minimum payments on all your debts.

5. In the first debt, the one with the smallest amount, dedicate all the savings and extra money obtained in the previous steps.

6. Once this debt is over, it goes on to the next one. And so on.

The Tsunami Method is about sorting your debts in the order that YOU CREATE. What is the debt that bothers you the most? The purchase of the last console? That's where you start cleaning up debts.

opt calmly for a debt consolidation loan, to get out now and immediately. A personal loan that is specifically used to combine multiple debts into a single monthly payment. Get that loan and use the funds you receive to pay off multiple debts of the same type. The advantages are that it simplifies the repayment, reducing it to an invoice, as well as the rate applied to the debt, which gives you for saving money. Another reduction is that of the monthly payment, although there are also fixed ones, it makes the payment of the debt more efficient. And how do I end up using that wonder? You apply for a loan in an amount that covers all the debts you want to consolidate. Once approved, the loan funds are distributed to pay off all those debts. So, all you have left is this loan to pay off.

Debts and Work

If you are in the credit bureaus of your country as a debtor, it is the first thing that certain employers will do to verify before hiring personnel, that the candidates do not appear in the credit bureaus. They do it to know that their next workers are not defaulters or bad payers.

Debts and health:

According to some news reports, as our debt grows, our health weakens. Even researchers are in the phase of trying to map the pattern of association accurately.

For example, a study of 900 adults in Ohio, United States, found that credit card debt and the stress of that debt were associated with poor health. But the investigators couldn't prove their causality. One of the researchers stated that "many of the major life events that can result in indebtedness (loss of employment, divorce, etc.) can also independently impact health, so it is important to separate those paths and trajectories.

A European Public Health journal stated that "indebted adults are three times more likely to have a common mental disorder than adults without debt. So, for your well-being, live a healthy and positive lifestyle, you'll be in such good physical and mental shape that it will represent a reduction in medical expenses and a positive outlook on life that helps you have good financial habits.

I want to emphasize changing the behavior that led us to this. **Even winning the lottery can't solve your problems if you don't learn to spend less than you have.** Here's how it shows: If you have $20,000 in credit card debt, don't take out a $25,000 loan to pay off that debt and buy things you don't need, giving a false appearance. Did you go into debt because you lost your job? Okay. [Chuckles] Once you get out of debt, create an emergency fund so that it doesn't happen to you again and part of the change is to say NO: NO to meaningless spending, NO to debt, NO to more credit while you're in the process of recovering, NO to going out at night, NO to additional credit cards.

Wake up early: It sounds like a cliché phrase, but it's not, in fact, many millionaires wake up before you do. One example is Tim Cook, who wakes up at 4:00 a.m., attends 700-800 mails a day and exercises in the gym before going to the office to be one of the first to arrive. The trick is to fall asleep in a good mood, get up very early and exercise.

As an interesting fact to keep in mind: After the death of a relative, you have to find out whether the deceased left outstanding debts to the banking system or to the State. To do this, you must process the death certificate of the deceased and contact your country's risk center to find out if there is an account with a bank. If the deceased person has a pending obligation such as a mortgage loan or long-term vehicle, the debt is inherited and it is the family members who must assume the payment, although it is important to determine that the bank can only collect the inheritance from the inheritance left by the deceased and not from their personal property. And anticipating this type of situation, most banks and municipal savings banks have tax deductible insurance, which exempts heirs from paying the balance of the credit requested. It should be noted that this insurance is activated as long as the deceased has been up to date in their payments, because if there are late payments, yes or yes should be canceled.

Conclusion

You decide to face the debt

If you suffer a change in your economic situation, such as a dismissal or a halt in your passive income, approach your bank to inform them of the problem before the payment is due and to be able to negotiate a solution. Don't ever be quiet.

Not everything is lost when you go into debt. When you see that your savings are decreasing and you are still in debt, think cold, that you don't win the emotion, you win it, calculating income, expenses, debts and assets, and with that baggage, you will empower yourself and you will turn to your financial advisor to guide you and do everything possible so that you and your bank are in good payment terms.

Arianna Huffington's second book was rejected by 36 publishers before it was published. Reading their story, I was perplexed, believing that for a few errors I was taken from the editorial boards. And now I see that they make worse mistakes in my workplace and I can't stand a very enjoyed giggle while I prepare this book so that you, reader, don't fall into the errors.

Another inspiration I found is Henry Ford, because before building his empire he founded the Detroit

Automobile Company, which failed after two years of operation and with only 20 cars built. After a good while, it could resurface with the brand we know today.

I suppose this couple of examples must have happened what we did with the debts and the imminent failure: worries, anxieties, thinking that you can seize everything and you will not have a hole to fall dead.

That happens if you remain silent and begin to evade your monetary responsibilities. Hey, all right, you feel guilty about spending part of your salary on that delicious chocolate, on that attractive salty dessert and you paid it with plastic money again. Well, be aware that a few more whims and you'll be on the street bald, with one hand forward and one back. Lose the fear of debt because if you think about it financially, the debt will work in your favor. So, grab paper and pencil, sit at your desk and draw up the bills and you'll see that you spend a lot and save little.

Now that you know the 50-30-20 technique, don't delay any longer and do it. And if the debts invade you, you know that the function of the financial advisor is to advise, to see the light at the end of the tunnel, and that you are also willing to pay on time and seek more income to fulfill your word.

Remember I mentioned my late professor at the beginning of the chapter? Well, he was a man who had worked and generated debts at the same time: instruments of work, family, property and insurance education for his own. Journalist, publicist, became part of the communication team of the Presidency of the Council of Ministers. With all the experience he had, he wasn't content to be just another communicator. To generate more income, he studied to become a wine taster, and his dream of opening an Italian pasta shop came true. I respect him because he was the first to warn me that the race was somehow very ungrateful. He spoke it with first-hand knowledge. He was so good at press, they pushed him aside. He was so good at dictating the course he was taking at the university that two more classrooms were opened for him to dictate, that internal movements of some professors made him to one side of the courses. He chose to correct texts in order to have an income and thus give life to the adventure of wine and pasta restaurant. Of course, he had debts like he said, but this didn't make him give up. Rather, it was death so stubborn that it made him one side of life to take him to his side.

The hair salon-bazaar-bookstore was in decline, and my mother had no better idea than to borrow money from the sister of a friend of hers. The lady was literally like the bank, but as we said above, even the bank gives you opportunities. My mother apparently did not take advantage of the few chances that this lender gave her, which when she saw that my mother did not pay the debt, began to pursue her, harass her in the battered business and not getting an answer, as I could not send her to jail for debts, chose to seize my father's car, marital property. That's where my mom reacted and reconciled a payment schedule so she could pay off the debt as soon as possible. Yes, they reconciled and I never saw the lady again, but it made my mother smarter and more business savvy.

So, don't be anxious if you have a debt that you think is priceless right now. Looking for solutions, you'll find them.

As a last case, I would like to comment on the debt in which my best friend from the university slipped away. Since he earned well enough in his previous job, he traveled twice to Mexico to visit his partner. As you may know, air travel and tours generate an incredible expense. He was just beginning to pay for the trip when he was taken out of his job. He had to apply for refinancing of the debt because if not, he could not continue to be solvent in the next job where he was paid the minimum wage. So, there are several examples, but you have the power to decide how to get out of your debts.

How to be Debt Free: Volume 3

A Proven Strategy to Take Control of Your Financial Freedom by Getting Rid of Debt, Loans, Student Loans Repayment, Credit Card Debt, Mortgages and More

By

Income Mastery

INTRODUCTION

This book can help you gain an advantage over those who have no prior knowledge of the whole world of work, money and insurance, as well as everything you need to survive in a world of broad job competition. You will realize that undertaking new projects is much easier than it seems when we approach them with the necessary expertise to solve all the unforeseen in a faster and safer way without many problems.

You will understand that the determination to pursue what you want to develop new skills is essential for all entrepreneurs entering the 21st century and how to take advantage of the risks to benefit you and achieve new goals.

You may not be able to manage your finances or maintain control of your financial freedom. In this book you will find the necessary bases you need to boost your dreams and attract a better performance in your company, not only to you, but to everyone around you.

So, start a journey to financial freedom and witness an almost instant improvement in your income to get out free of all your debts!

Chapter 1: If Money Doesn't Fall from Heaven... Where Does It Come From?

At some point in our lives we encounter millions of questions and doubts which, however silly and insignificant they may seem, hinder us in one way or another in moving forward and aspiring to fulfil our plans for the future. Perhaps also, sometimes we feel that seeking some advice or help will be the dumbest decision we can have and we venture into a totally unknown terrain, this is never recommended, therefore we may fall by innocent in situations that could have been avoided with a little more preparation.

In other cases, the opposite case can happen, when we are led by comments from people with bad intentions or no experience, who fill us with doubts and uncertainty, or many other questions that lead us to a great wall of frustrations that prevents us from knocking it down block by block to gain more security. All this first step causes us discomfort or the feeling of inability to achieve our final goal, we must not lose the goal and remain fixed with sight of the target. Some of the questions that arise in the process are sometimes similar to these below:

"Where can I get money?", "What is the best way to get money?", "How can I get financial stability?" "When can

I get financial security and well-being?", "What do I need to achieve it?", "How long will it take me to accomplish my goal?", "What do I do if it doesn't turn out the way I expected?", "What do I need insurance for?

Each and every one of these doubts never comes alone, they are accompanied by many other questions and insecurities that accumulate over time, but we manage to answer them in the moment. We will be forever pursuing that doubt, our goal will be different from the rest of the others and we think we may be doing something wrong, we feel at some point tied or committed not only to debts, but to fears, doubts and a completely non-existent economic independence, then, from one moment to another, we cannot fall asleep at night or acquire a feeling of restlessness in the mornings thanks to those decisions we want to make as soon as possible and does not occur.

Adding this to the above, we will always find the daily competition, both in the field of work and in different areas of our lives. Competition brings with its great advantages and disadvantages, but without a doubt they are good benchmarks that we must face even if we do not have the full certainty of getting out of them completely unharmed. Therefore, in the face of competition, initial preparation is essential, it makes things easier for us in these cases. There is no need to get stuck at this previous preparation, it will always be an important experience in any business or new financial plan you have in mind. Moving forward does not always mean going forward, you can stop and go back to better analyze all the possibilities you have in your hands, this gives you the advantage of feeling more confident and more secure against the risks that must be taken to get better benefits. We can never forget that wealth is not only a virtue referring to monetary acquisition, but that it also forms part of the whole process that is taken to arrive at it, to take charge and to be responsible for every minimum step that has to be faced. All these elements will allow us to assume the risks of investing knowing that without them we would not be able to talk about future benefits in the short or medium term.

If we start from the premise that money does not fall from the sky, if it were otherwise you would not find yourself between these lines right now or with the concern of achieving economic stability, because you would not require it, the best way is to face the situation and visualize the most favorable conditions for a venture, every step that you take, no matter how small they seem, are indispensable to achieve your goals as quickly as possible and you can't stop because at some point you think that this idea for the future is not feasible or is completely null and even impossible to accomplish, if you consider this at some point you just have to change your course a little bit, these mental blocks that only you can break them, don't lose the calm that while you're learning you're not failing, take a little time and breathe that when everything seems to be going wrong it's not too much to stop for a few seconds without losing your objective. To start with, you have to be clear that not everything is as difficult as it seems or as complicated as you were painted at some point, but quite the opposite, just know the right way to approach your dreams.

Good ideas and financial dreams are largely only limited by the people themselves because they lack imagination, self-confidence and the little capacity you have to consider thousands of possibilities that are in your favor, although, do not be confused, having good ideas does not ensure that you will achieve economic wellbeing just by thinking about them, it is about theory praxis this refers to that everything that you say you practice it in an assertive way, you can be a genius having unique, creative and innovative ideas with a high degree of entrepreneurship, but if you do not present the necessary tools, the organization and the discipline to materialize what you want can still exist a great probability of failing and failing in the attempt. That is to say, to have great ideas, you are not exempt from feeling doubts and even frustration that promote having thoughts of abandoning all that you have advanced until now, when this happens it is the right moment to stop and reflect.

Getting the income you need means venturing from the first moment into the big world of work, this world of work can start from doing jobs you never imagined to be part of something where it does not seem encouraging to continue, certainly such situations were not among your plans but can lead you through the experience gained and recognition of your own expectations, to something much better.

For this reason the positive and reflective being of your own labor situation will open marvelous doors to you, the possibilities are infinite no matter where you look at them, you should not limit yourself to any unforeseen situation and much less underestimate yourself to an unfavorable position that leads you to think that it escapes from your hands to revert or improve. Always no matter what, thinking cold before any decision is the best advice someone can give you, always keep your feet on the ground. Be alert to things that may change and never close to these changes. Everything has its margin of error and they are not exact, even more when the markets fluctuate from one moment to another, as well as when we depend on any job that has a monetary reward.

Not knowing where to start is completely normal and natural even though it may fill us with shame, take us away from our comfort zone and feel a little ignorant or incapable regarding some subject that we do not handle with complete security and confidence entering an unknown space such as the world of money and insurance (remember these words that we will develop later), is something that with only daring will become simpler with the passing of time, this arises only with a magic word that we will learn each time we continue trying with the passage of time that is "practice".

Everything can be a pleasant walk if only you propose it, the most intelligent thing is to detect the doubts that you have to go answering little by little each one of these taking us the necessary time so that everything is processed in the most suitable way and you can analyze it with more detail, remember that we all have a different time to carry out our projects, take this into consideration if among your plans you are not completely alone or if you develop it with someone else because all along this path we plan to conclude in a future that is as enriching as possible without many setbacks or exaggerated difficulties.

We are in a completely technological and digital era that with the ease and five minutes of your time you can, surfing the Internet as many times as you want, find numerous opportunities to acquire benefits and answer in a simpler way to some of these first questions we ask when we start a new project, we get a wide variety of answers, but not all these answers answer all our questions, do not meet most of our expectations or we feel dissatisfied with the desire to acquire much more than what we find and do not really know where to get it, we may start to feel down at some point by situations like these, but all this previous research gives us much more vital information that we did not have and strengthen us when it comes to undertake our best financial possibilities and taking risks safely. Having a stable base makes it easier to move forward (Read on to find out how to take safe risks).

As we begin the ideal economic path to achieve the dreamed independence that we all require in our lives will be embodied throughout this third volume, where we will try to answer each and every one of those questions regarding how to obtain money, insurance, advice and more, which can ensure and encourage you in the world of work to elucidate in a less complex and more understandable way this broad topic of business. It will help you take the first step to start your monetary freedom and financial well-being as soon as possible without dying in the attempt, on your way to the economic happiness you deserve.

Chapter 2: Formula to get money... easy, fast and safe?

This is the million-dollar question, your answer would solve absolutely all the problems that more than one of us is suffering at the moment, what is money and why we are here, is a delicate issue for some people and is not at all easy. We know perfectly well that money cannot buy happiness but it is better to cry driving a Ferrari and eating, than to go on foot and hungry, we all want, as we deserve, to know the answer to this question and many more. There is nothing we would love more than to be able to find the ideal route with the naked eye as if it were a pill that would be prescribed in any doctor's office and just going to the pharmacy on the corner would be there the answer to where is that great opportunity that is made exclusively for you and thus be able to earn more than an extra a month.

As much as you don't believe it, this opportunity is right in front of your nose and you can't see it even if you propose it, as described and illustrated by the author Antonie de Saint-Exupéry in his famous children's story called "The little prince" in which this beautiful story also gives us a lot of wisdom, moving away from the thoughts so gridded in one of its chapters teaches us that "The essential is invisible to the eyes" and it is in this thought that we must be governed to begin with because there are not one, but, multiple ways in which we can obtain something feasible that becomes more than a push to improve our quality of life in the near future.

However it is true that some people require much more effort and time than others to advance their goals and not all projects will be handled in the same way or communicate with the same language but in the end are a great complement to carry them out, this experience is beneficial if you are looking for a new job or you are thinking about changing jobs and open to new choices that gives you the ability to explore those options with more freedom, as there are multiple platforms, not only on the Internet, you can find in those that offer you millions of choices to provide a service in exchange for another depending on what are your best qualities and what is your previous experience both academic and work.

Safe, easy and fast.

Before going deeper into the various jobs we can acquire it is important to bear in mind that according to the real Spanish academy known by the acronym RAE one of the meanings attributed to work is "Difficulty, impediment or prejudice" certainly many of us identify work with those words and on various occasions it is true and we even live it in our own flesh, there is no job that is safe and many times we sacrifice much of our lives in an environment that does not enrich us, nor deserves it, we end up feeling lost, used, frustrated and undervalued by our employers.

There is no easy job and there is nothing to discourage us for this, on the contrary, the idea is to find the perfect turn where to put it in our favor, the best job, no doubt, is that in which you unwrap in a comfortable and quiet way, although on many occasions you will find yourself with situations that will make you leave your comfort zone but you must know that you can with each of the challenges that you put and get your best virtues that can help you get afloat and get out of a victorious way where you feel proud and in accordance with what you make proud and conform to what you do; one of Confucius' famous phrases that tells us about this is the following: "Choose a job that you are passionate about and you will not have to work a single day of your life" by enjoying what you do all the benefits you can get from it will always be profit and no loss.

Quick jobs give you quick profits but ephemeral this you can understand better through this simple formula:

Profits = (Time x Effort)

Determination

Plan it this way, if the earnings is the final result you want to get, you have to apply three more data that will be fundamental to have a reliable result and this does not change to be a false positive that we do not expect, complicating everything, and this begins to compete with our pace of work or life. I will explain it to you in this simpler way, time is indispensable not only to carry out your daily activities, but, you must acquire a free time that is completely dedicated to start the search for income with the activity that you are going to carry out, regardless of which it is, it will help you to obtain that compensation that you need, all you sow will be what you will be able to reap at the end. At this point is where the fun of the equation begins, the time for the effort that you put, depending on the determination that you have will be proportional to the final result, if your determination is big enough applying the two previous data is the formula for success.

Self-Employment

Internet gives us information about a wide range of independent jobs where we have the opportunity to develop in the way you want, as well as having the great possibility and advantage of finding millions of platforms where you can explore a large number of offers to get the one that best suits your pace of life, while this gives you the compensation that you consider best according to your skills.

Before explaining all the job possibilities that exist it is vital to understand that there is an active and passive income, you may wonder what this is but it is very simple. First, let's define what an asset is. This is an accounting term that is used to call all those goods, materials and real estate that comprises a person or company in its possession. But what is an active income? The active income is the money you receive through a job that requires your time, dedication and effort, in short, you are paid for the time invested in which you perform an activity they require, while the passive income is just the opposite, are income obtained without requiring any of your time and these are increasing progressively while you do not dedicate anything and can include your time to other types of projects.

Passive income is what will give you the true economic freedom you yearn for as well as being the biggest secret of many multimillionaire businessmen or at least the way in which they managed to acquire the economic status that they continue to maintain despite the weather. Even many famous artists as they get older maintain the same rhythm of life thanks to royalties for the works done that still have a great profit, but of course, this can only be achieved after obtaining active income, of course, whether we want it or not, we cannot skip this step, remember that in order to achieve our goal we start with a steady step at a time.

Among some of the options that may be feasible online you can get the advantage of staying in the comfort of your room without the complications of the jobs, there are many but it will always depend on the skills you have. The digital marketing for example, is one of them, if you consider yourself good in the advertising of sale these are paid by means of a percentage of commissions; another option is if you have some skill, like drawing, selling your art and what you know how to do on the Internet can open many doors.

Remember that some opportunities can be deceptive, in many places on the Internet you sell courses and training on how to venture into these platforms and earn money quickly and easily, but this is not true, much of these courses do not give you truthful or secure information, or invite you to invest money without prior knowledge of and with or without malicious intent you can lose it, you must always keep in mind that this fluctuates.

Some spend their time in online sales but if you don't make an investment and just sell your belongings you will end up worse than you started. The easy in many opportunities is not the best way to go.

From another point of view if you are much more traditional or do not feel comfortable with this time of employment, there are always part-time or full-time possibilities that you can get and you are much more comfortable. Comfort is important but do not be afraid to get out of it when necessary, if you want to move forward and achieve goals that you have never achieved you will have to have actions you have never done, always be active in an activity that gives you economic benefits is the best way to start the path to independence and freedom, not only mental or emotional, but the goal is not only to have benefits to see them completely, you have to know how to manage, give you tastes is the healthiest and most important thing, always reward you for each progress to enjoy the fruits obtained.

Now, if you have a bad management of your assets, which are ultimately the resources obtained, by wasting these resources that can be translated into goods or cash that are not well managed in a coherent way will end up being wasted, and you only get not even to have to invest in some productive project, not to satisfy your basic needs, much less to see the true progress you may have projected over time and that most of these times we end up enslaved by unsatisfactory work to pay the bills, as a result we would end up becoming unsatisfied people, tired and trapped in the same story of unfulfilled dreams. Without a doubt, this situation influences the economic development of each one of us, even more so when our objectives are to be part of a creative and fun business that will always make us prosper, that will allow us to be and feel sustainable and independent and, above all, completely happy with what we do.

Chapter 3: Transforming Weakness into Strength

We all have some weakness that makes us feel insecure and unable to achieve certain goals in our lives, but we must bear in mind that weakness is nothing more than ignorance about some step we take, you'll wonder what they relate to, do not worry, there is no exact manual in which we can resort and tell us step by step what to follow to get what we want and if you find it there is no security that covers each of all the setbacks that may arise at some unforeseen time, there is no exact formula for everything, the idea of this is that you can adapt to the needs you have and cover them in the best possible way. If there were such a facility to solve any problem the weaknesses would not be taken as something of such gravity and certainly it is not, the weakness is only something transitory that can be transformed into a fortress in a simple and accessible way as knowledge is to the unknown.

Let's represent this with some simple formulas, remember that to solve any type of obstacle you only have to have a little imagination and determination, have a square thought, making allegory to the "Little Prince", they prevent us from visualizing innovative solutions, if we do not feel satisfied with the way in which some situations are presented this will make it difficult to create a new proposal to overcome this difficulty satisfactorily, specifically weakness in most cases is the direct result of ignorance and correct knowledge will represent the answer to all these problems:

Weakness = Ignorance

Ignorance = Knowledge

When we cross out the first three letters of the word ignorance we have as a result knowledge and this does not only apply in this case, but in many others such as disinterest in interest, carelessness in concern and demotivation in motivation. These three previous examples show us that if we cross out everything that does not allow us to prosper and stop us, when we detect what is the weakness we have, we obtain that this becomes the main knowledge to be able to change it, to get rid of the insecurity that gives us the weakness and thus transform it into one more strength.

A clear example is when we begin to form part of a company or we begin a new work or project that we have, always there will be weaknesses without importing that this is completely normal, but these are only by the lack of information in the area that we approached, not to know principally how to do it having the necessary resources for its achievement, if you get the resources but do not know how to transform them into the final product is the main weakness, so in many companies implement the trainings before starting, they show not only interest, but, the capacity of perseverance that has the future employee so that this is not a weakness at the time of performing the job, in these trainings provide the necessary structure of what to do and how to do it.

Knowledge = Strength =/ Ignorance

Knowledge is equal to strength and different from ignorance, if we obtain knowledge weakness will not exist, will become a strength because you know how to act and how you will carry out that difficulty at the time it arises. When there are only strengths, it is the moment when opportunities arise and you are able to acquire many more strengths.

We are all exposed to catastrophic and uncertain situations and most of us do not know how to handle them, if you are an enterprising person you can take this to your advantage and never see it as an obstacle. If knowing what you don't handle and informing others in your environment using your strengths can educate and help build the strength of others in your work environment, with this you can get more satisfying and important results in your income.

Chapter 4: Insurance... Planned Risks?

When we talk about security, we can have two approaches, these are very different from each other, although both are closely related to each other. Then we can refer in principle to the feeling of security as a basic instinct that we acquire by obtaining some type of object that covers a basic need, reducing our risks of survival, making our daily activities easier and bearable; on the other hand, the second approach is that which gives the security offered by multiple insurers against a risk or event that may occur in the future, whether this is uncertain and independent of the will of the insured without being able to prevent it from happening, then we will develop both approaches from the points of view described above.

Safety as a basic instinct.

The need for security is a force that dominates all spheres of our lives, for all people, regardless of our type of work venture or our lifestyle, from the very moment we begin the path to the economic well-being we desire, that sense of security is required to move forward. If we do not feel safe before the actions that we take, in any moment we will have the desire to abandon or to retire, in this way the insecurity prevents us from taking the best decisions for any enterprise, so much by the fear to the unknown as the lack of tools to confront and to overcome the fears that can be emerging. The above can affect the decision making at a new opportunity, can even make us walk away without thinking twice, this is a clear and obvious error of what many of us commit throughout our lives.

For this same reason, it is of vital priority in all work that we do or that we carry out, as in the undertakings, that we propose to satisfy the necessary security, therefore this aspect should not be neglected in the different aspects of our daily life as work. This makes us reiterate that safety is a basic instinct that we must try to cover in the first instance, as important as the physiological needs of every human being are as important as eating or sleeping. I will explain it to you in this way, one of the first needs that we need to have is that of emotional, perhaps even the most important. If we do not feel sure of ourselves and of being able to achieve any obstacle, we will be stuck in the mediocrity of the word "I cannot" and I do not assure you that we will not even get to the corner with this thought.

However, beyond the emotional security to which we refer, there are other types of security that we require, such as economic security, legal security, health security, among many others. There is therefore a broad spectrum to refer to when talking about security, but that does not mean that we should take it for granted that they are covered in all their aspects without our due attention.

It could be the case that, although we have enough emotional security that has allowed us to guarantee an economic security, this does not guarantee that we can doubt the effective response to a situation of risk, especially to guarantee legal services, doctors who may be required, for example the legal need is of great interest to every contract we make, not having to see these as a simple sheet of signed paper that has no real value, to properly process the notarized certification of them, will provide us with a greater stability in our economic security. The latter is not only given by the labor expertise you present or how good you are at generating income, but also by your ability to make decisions that intelligently protect the assets and ultimately the entire undertaking.

Before this we can see that we are able to avoid certain events with a good organization. We can also respond to certain events in an appropriate way when we face some of these problems. Prevention is important in any event we enter. To get rid of events that can happen just because they are negative doesn't lead you to avoid them or just because you don't think about them, there is no possibility that they will happen. Not creating a reserve plan to deal with these damages can be the formula that leads us to failure on many occasions.

This is also how a good management of the resources you have in your power and a good saving of capital, allows us to acquire a sustainable basis for facing a safe risk, this important point will be developed in more detail in the next chapter. It is always recommended to have a reliable insurance company that allows us to have the certainty that in any moment of danger you can really count on something certain and tangible that helps you not to have significant losses in your investment and that directs you to abandon the projects that you carry out thus strengthening the general feeling of security that we require to have.

Security in the face of events or facts.

When we are in economic progress there are some threats that can harm and be unfavorable in our economy, this is where the work of the insurers enters, they are responsible for providing optimal coverage to certain kinds of risks that may present the assets of a person or their own integrity, all this through fees or also known and called premiums paid, which is nothing more than the costs of insurance. These premiums are those that provide the security to be able to solve the problem at the moment that an incident or loss occurs or becomes present that puts at risk the investment and even the integrity of the venture. It is necessary to keep in mind when obtaining an insurance that you are not exempt or prevents this risk from happening, but thanks to this the economic losses you suffer when presenting them can be compensated.

But really the question is: What are the risks, these must be understood as the possibility that there is a fact that occurs that in many occasions we ignore for lack of information and these bring unfavorable economic repercussions directly to the assets that you have, are damages caused out of your own will and desire that in many occasions we cannot control, as it is, for example, an unforeseen climatic event such as a flood, a fire or thefts incurred by third parties outside our control.

It is here that we must know that insurers are very specific as to the coverage that they can offer, this depends on the fact to occur, have certain parameters that must meet, one of these is that this must be an event in time future, not current, or past, cannot have happened in the past or is happening at present, the existence of risk is the essential thing that must occur to be able to obtain insurance, these events that occur in the future cannot occur by the liability of the insured. In short, any damage caused regardless of the loss, the insurer is not responsible, must be an event entirely occurred by chance, also add that the type of damage that is caused must be defined, such as a theft or a fire occurred, do not fully cover all the risks you can run, finally, only if the damage causes a financial loss and this does not serve as profit for the insured, if it meets all these parameters will be covered by insurance.

Now, I am going to describe to you and make known the different insurance modalities that can offer the companies dedicated to this branch, this with the purpose that you always take into account that according to the size of the investment and the type of enterprise that you make, to insure your investment is a factor to be taken into account to avoid a partial or total loss in case of an unforeseen or fortuitous and unexpected situation. This will depend on your drive, your self-confidence, the study of opportunities as well as the advantages and disadvantages of the market you will enter.

Types of insurance.

There is a wide diversity when we talk about the types of insurance, this exists for each different type of future risk that we may present at some point in our lives, these are divided into three different classifications. The first one we will explain next will be the insurance called "**personal insurance**", this kind of insurance offers coverage to the damage that affects the individual. This means things that can endanger the well-being and integrity and even the life of the insured. This insurance includes life, sickness and accident insurance. This is followed by "**risk insurance**" which involves direct damage to our goods, causing great economic losses, and finally, the so-called "**multi-risk insurance**" which will be explained in more detail at the end of this chapter.

Personal insurance

The life insurance or personal insurance have the work and responsibility to respond to an event that endangers our integrity as an individual, they are responsible for indemnifying us and protecting us from an unforeseen event. They have the duty to cover not only the death of the insured person, but also the survival of the insured person. This survival implies having a savings which has been progressively paid to the insurer so that at the time of retirement or incapacitation this is granted to the insured. This type of insurance presents guarantees that cover both life and death.

Health insurance, or also known as health and accident insurance, is the best known and undoubtedly the most recurrent. These insurances give you a general evaluation and study your life years, thus establishing a stipulated amount of the value of your life, in addition to this they establish amounts for each pathology that you may present as for example arterial hypertension, diabetes or some metabolic problem that you possess. Health insurance is more widely used in the event of unforeseen accidents when both specialized and simple surgical intervention is required. If you do not present insurance, the costs of the procedures are very high and very unprofitable but possessing this kind of security is the most reliable way to bear these expenses when they occur.

Damage insurance

Unlike personal insurances, these are responsible for compensating all the damages that cause economic losses on an insured material good, compensating with a percentage to be able to recover these losses suffered by the breakdown, theft or damage of the same. Insurance companies are responsible for the material goods presented by the insured and these objects in turn present an objective value, if they do not have it, it is not a good that can be insured as it requires a monetary value and not only sentimental, this can be from a property, a vehicle, construction projects, to merchandise purchased for an investment.

Multi-risk insurance

This last class of insurance is a very particular insurance, different from the rest. This class of insurance includes policies that cover a wide variety of risks to which a specific activity or material insured may be committed. These risks are based on material objects and goods as well as patrimonial and personal, in this case the best-known examples of these insurances are the well-known household insurances, commercial insurances, independently of these being of a small or medium enterprise. All this includes and covers in a single insurance contract with coverage to various incidents or events such as fires, robberies, damages caused by others, civil liability or accidents of third parties.

Finally, it must be emphasized that depending on the venture you own, you must opt for insurance and if your venture is large, it is even more recommendable and favorable to require one and be insured because this guarantees that when catastrophe situations occur, a partial or complete loss of investment does not occur in the worst case scenario. It is not the same to go for the sure thing to be sure, if the conditions given to keep the invested capital are not found they can have complete losses, your debts will increase and you will not be able to obtain the economic freedom that you want to reach. It is necessary to take into account other aspects besides work, such as emotional aspects. According to the needs you present, it will be the best insurance you require when facing an event that involves a risk.

Chapter 5: Achieving goals requires borrowing and taking risks.

When you invest money to take control of your financial freedom we always choose the option that gives us the greatest economic security possible, now we make much clearer what are the economic risks that can happen and how insurers can provide compensation not only emotional, but also economic, covering some financial loss for an unforeseen future, but many of the risks not supported by an insurer are those taken at the time when we venture to regain administrative control of our income and what we implement so that these grow as time goes by. However, these risks still have the probability of causing us to lose some or all of our investment, but if we don't, we move further and further away from the hope of meeting the goals we set for ourselves.

When it comes to assuming a risk, expertise will be essential when we are at the moment of making the decision in the face of a financial risk. To reach the goal we desire, anyone can have this ability, with it we will solve in a much simpler way, with speed and in a competent way, problems no matter the obstacle imposed that this has. In order to develop this ability we have to put into practice the experience gained throughout our lives, this may be a theoretical learning, some experience or something you have seen at some point and be able to replicate it not in all cases the same way but with satisfactory results.

Acquiring a risk that rewards us much more than our minimum profit limit is what we all want, but do not take these risks lightly, a very simple example is:

When you purchase a vehicle using a credit, you are assuming a risk. To have a car is indispensable for any rhythm of life but if this is used during the time that the credit is still cancelled. If it's not used for personal use, if it's not cleverly affiliated with a company, you can have the expenses you have canceled out on their own, but how do you do this? One idea is to affiliate it as Uber, you will run an investment risk to begin with but this can be feasible to compensate your economic income with the costs that month by month you must make yourself responsible for canceling, in addition to all the interests that brings with it, there are multiple insurance companies that can offer you an insurance to prevent any damage that the vehicle can present and thus support you not to have economic losses by unforeseen events.

Be objective, direct and clear in each and every one of your plans. When you get loans and you show that with all your income you can take charge of more benefits, they will always call you and offer you even more than you really need, that happens thanks to the so-called positive credit, but we cannot be dazzled by the amount of proposals no matter how amazing what they offer us and they do not have the security of providing us with an economic benefit. Approaching all our actions responsibly will enable us to reach our final goal. Therefore, the expertise obtained in the processing, management and organization of investments and income will undoubtedly make the difference in each venture you propose.

Because of the above, skill is a skill that allows you to handle a problem in alternate ways, for example:

Through what is known as cultural transmission, as we grow, we soak up completely new information, from learning to walk, talk and communicate, in this primary stage to knowing what to do and how to respond to personal and social environment requirements, in the second stage of the learning process. However, in the face of each new need that arises and deserves to be solved, this learning process will bear fruit over time, experiences lived and lessons learned become part of us, so we can reach a point where we will respond to certain situations in a natural way, and even by experience do so in a different way but with the same or better results.

We refer to the required expertise that has to be obtained beforehand through experience, as it is a fact that economic independence does not come in a cereal box and there is no financial godmother who will grant you the stability and independence you need just by waving a small magic wand, if it were this way we would not spend our time or money planning projects that can lead us to be closer and closer to economic stability and freedom. Sometimes we compare this search as similar or equal to the task of finding a needle in a haystack.

That's why, recognizing our previous experience as a significant tool allows you to visualize that giving your best will make you receive more and more benefits. The more effort and dedication in learning and developing tools and skills that translate into expertise, the greater the likelihood of reward and sometimes increased. The effort pays off but it depends on how much you have dedicated in the beginning; nothing is free and everything that comes fast in the same way flows and disappears. The time invested is never wasted, even if you don't get what you want, we gain experience and this will be an important part of the expertise.

Chapter 6: Four "D's" that can help you get financial freedom.

There are many qualities that are essential when starting an ideal economic path, but what do we call an ideal economic path? Very easy, it is a question of undertaking the search for new opportunities where we can enrich ourselves economically, maintaining a progressive stability for a greater monetary benefit, where our best profile must stand out before any other weakness to favor us and make us useful to what we need, but if we feel a little lost and we need to know or know what can help us to impel us or which are the best aspects when facing the labor competition, On the contrary, when we find ourselves in such a competitive world we do not lower the quality of our product or the work we do. On the contrary, what we try to do is progressively increase the quality until it becomes the favorite product of all our consumers.

Exploring the alternatives that can be presented to obtain the so desired financial freedom it makes me coherent to present you with these "D" boxes, which are no more than the guide that you will get through those key words, which I think are tools that you should exercise to initiate or structure your financial freedom even better.

The four "D's" I refer to are nothing more than determination, dedication, direction and discipline. Each one of them implies by itself a wide process of personal commitment, but all together without any doubt they will contribute a firm base to your personal growth and of course an economic independence to the height of your commitment. Without further ado, these are the four D's:

Determination:

Determination is nothing more than setting objectives, pointing out the defects and virtues that may or may not present a project to be able to develop it in an organized way. Guiding the key steps needed to reach an end. Determination gives us a feeling of greater security, but this is also an injection of passion, of daring, if something can be achieved it will be thanks to the determination to achieve it, so we must also know that within determination there is something called self-determination. Being self-determined and being able to make independent decisions from comments that may influence it, if you consider it to be the best way to act will be so no matter what may happen. This will undoubtedly make you grow as a person making you feel more and more owner of your destiny.

But determination and self-determination do not go alone, on the other hand there is determinism which is a much more philosophical thought, it is the kind of positive thought for labor entrepreneurship, it states that all events that may happen in the future will depend on the decisions you make and these will have consequences that can positively influence your performance. This determinism must not be square, nor must it be kept inert. There is always the influence of unpredictable events by chance and this is why we must take the necessary precautions to fight them by means of planned risks.

Dedication:

Dedication is closely linked to time and effort. Throughout this volume we have repeated the word time and effort, which is nothing more than the exclusive dedication that we have in front of the economic spheres to achieve financial freedom. If we have exclusive dedication to what we want to obtain it will be more evident to achieve it since we link ourselves completely in the activities that we carry out, these will be centered to the future benefit that we can obtain.

Therefore, as in the different stages of our growth, it was necessary to dedicate time and effort to learn to speak, then to communicate in an assertive way, how to learn different means that today allow you to communicate in the same way. The good use of that time dedicated to the strengthening and development of your physical and mental capacities will make the difference before the opportunities and your capacity to reach them until making them yours as part of your learning process.

Address

The direction is the direction we take and depending on which direction we take it will also lead us to the success we desire. It is about orienting the actions of your labor undertaking to a certain end, set goals, make decisions and thus guide you to what you want to obtain. If you are part of a company or you are starting one, you have to keep in mind that not only must have the address of the person who directs it, on the contrary, a good address allows all those who participate in the company to be part of it. The same case occurs in any human conglomerate. To say that there is a good direction is to have proven to be clear and efficient, thus allowing everyone to know very well what it should do, where to go and what actions to take in the event of any requirement or eventuality.

This is how we can ensure that the success of a good management is in making all members of a company or project of any kind are involved in all aspects of it, and therefore, to the extent that everyone is involved forms a sense of belonging and this makes it flow progressively towards the goal. It has to be considered at the same time that to design strategies with clear objectives allows to organize appropriate tactics that take us to reach the final end that is not more than the well-being and benefit of all the involved.

Discipline:

Last but not least, we have discipline. When talking about discipline, one does not only refer to behavior, but also to the fact that discipline requires an appropriate and positive attitude. The attitude can be translated as the way, the energy and even the desire that are externalized and assumed at the time of taking the leading role and deepening in the needs of any type of project.

At the same time, discipline is governed by certain types of codes, among other steps to point out two of the most important that must be taken into account and fully complied with to ensure the faithful achievement of your objectives. The first is the duty to comply punctually with work schedules and the second is to devote every day at a certain time to improve a skill. The latter is known as self-discipline, which is a structure formed by a series of steps and attitudes that we carry out in a constant manner.

After having described and pointed out to you the four "D's" that will be able to gestate the foundations of your economic independence and of great value for your personal development, taking attention and proposing to make them an active part of your life will show you more and more the benefit of them. Financial stability is not achieved by antonomasia alone, it will require you to lend it commitment and constancy.

We can conclude that the objective that we set ourselves at the beginning of this path, to orient the four "D's", is to understand that although they may be similar, each one has a different important approach that influences us. If we are determined to achieve an objective but do not have the right direction, we may deviate from the objective and encounter other barriers that prevent us from moving forward. On the other hand, if we have a clear direction but lack dedication and discipline, we find ourselves stuck and cannot visualize the progress we have because we do not have the necessary focus.

For this reason, we must maintain a balance. If we have the right direction, the determination to make decisions and face setbacks with dedication and discipline, we will have the necessary basis to start any kind of opportunity without the need to abandon and successfully achieve our objectives.

CONCLUSION

After having tackled the different topics throughout this third volume, where each one of them highlights an important aspect that has as its main objective to allow us to fulfill all our projects in the future, only if we are able to put them into practice and they do not remain just between these lines, because it not only helps us to enrich ourselves with a wide variety of advice and knowledge that may be that we did not have in the beginning or did not understand them completely, but thanks to all this we can conclude and refer in the following way to each one of the postulates mentioned before:

The effort is the first aspect that we talked about in the first chapter and this is not by chance that this is there. When we venture into a completely unknown world and are completely new at this, we will always have stumbles, doubts, fears and a number of negative thoughts that will only fuel the desire to give up. This is where the effort comes in, no matter how many times we fall and although this attracts not at all favorable economic repercussions, the effort to win is the solution to find that opportunity in which we will develop only with time, everything is a daily learning and no matter what, even the unfavorable does not end up being like that completely, because when it happens again we know how to handle ourselves in front of them and know which face to put on.

Another important aspect in every project undertaken is that we must finish it, even if we are sure that it will not have the same fruits that in the beginning were planned to obtain or that even they deserve. Moreover, when the abandonment of a project not only leaves the bad taste of defeat in the mouth, it also makes see that all the time, effort and of course investment made is translated into a total loss. Therefore, it is essential to take each project to the end, the whole process will make you grow a little more and is adding to your experience. Finishing a project or a goal shows us what we are capable of, this can open doors to new and better opportunities where you feel more comfortable and secure than you do but despite this you show that no matter what is presented since you can take care of it.

The time is not only the second aspect that we treat in the second postulate, but like the previous one it is a parameter that has to be even considered as the first of all, this is translated in a simple way: if you don't have time to make what you want, it won't materialize. As true as it is: time is money. In this sense we have that the equation effort and time used in its maximum expression will rise to its maximum power if we are able to achieve our financial goals and achieve the economic stability required to achieve financial freedom. The more time you dedicate and even be exclusive, you can progressively get the economic compensation and you will have there the source of your resources to advance to new and better plans for the future.

In this sense, as nothing is static and inert in a place, even so are our own weaknesses, even though as we move forward it seems that we can find that we have many more weaknesses than we thought, there lies the time to devote to your weaknesses to know them with the firm intention of transforming them into new strengths. In this way we can avoid stagnation, it is an energy that therefore we must let flow. At this point we can take as an example the first two laws of thermodynamics which could well refer to the content of the third chapter. Weaknesses are not destroyed but transformed and they can never become weaknesses again because they change part of what was, is no longer found, and it is what transforms this into fortresses. Let's remember that weakness is only the ignorance that we have to not know how to deal with something in particular. If we add this to the two previous aspects, we obtain that if we have exclusivity of time, effort and the weaknesses changed to strengths, we assure ourselves even more the economic success.

With regard to security and the need we have for it in all its expressions, we now better understand that security is not just a sensation and a basic need, if it does not go much further, we begin with the emotional security we develop in the progress of learning and knowledge, in addition to the enormous network of security needs that we must know and foresee in any undertaking until we know the security that insurance companies can offer us against future, uncertain and independent risks, to our own security that entails economic losses and that for each risk there are different insurance classifications that indemnify us and give us the opportunity, in the event of any unforeseen event, not to lose completely or partially our investment. With this we can continue to develop our goal, time, effort and strengths along with the security that gives us the opportunity not only to conclude our projects, but to face other opportunities.

The issue of risks was also addressed, mentioning them as part of the process and the vastness of the decisions that must be taken. These always carry a margin of error, therefore, it is worth noting that the most famous entrepreneurs began taking risks, no doubt, as all of us were not exempt from not happening to them but only with expertise, practice and good decision making could reach the point of achieving passive income. This prompted them to achieve financial freedom. They apply everything in the process to obtain much more beneficial results and despite this they still run to raise even more, not only their income but also their personal growth, proving to themselves that they can solve a difficulty from the perspective that there are always multiple alternatives but only one will be the most convenient.

To finish we have, that if you present effort in what you do, you invest time, you present strengths that are increasing little by little, you have a security, not only emotional but also financial, you take the risks in a planned way, you add to all this the four "D", determination, dedication, direction and discipline there will not be an objective that we cannot fulfill and the financial freedom will come to you, but this freedom is not something static. Progressively, we must continue over and over again to put into practice everything we learned in this book in order to maintain not only our status quo, but also economic well-being and financial freedom. It is worth emphasizing the above for the development of the four "D's", maintaining the balance between these four premises will allow you to develop characteristics that will lead you to successfully achieve the objectives set.

www.ingramcontent.com/pod-product-compliance
Lightning Source LLC
Chambersburg PA
CBHW071703210326
41597CB00017B/2308